MOMENTS WITHOUT NAMES

BOOKS BY MORTON MARCUS

POETRY

Origins (Kayak, 1969)

Where the Oceans Cover Us (Capra, 1972)

The Santa Cruz Mountain Poems (Capra, 1972)

*The Armies Encamped in the Fields Beyond
The Unfinished Avenues: Prose Poems* (Jazz Press, 1977)

*Big Winds, Glass Mornings, Shadows Cast by Stars:
Poems, 1972-1980* (Jazz Press, 1980)

Pages From a Scrapbook of Immigrants
(Coffee House, 1988)

When People Could Fly: Prose Poems (Hanging Loose, 1997)

Moments Without Names: Selected Prose Poems
(White Pine Press, 2002)

Shouting Down the Silence (Creative Arts Book Company, 2002)

FICTION

The Brezhnev Memo (Dell/Delacorte, 1981)

MOMENTS WITHOUT NAMES

NEW & SELECTED
PROSE POEMS

BY
MORTON MARCUS

WHITE PINE PRESS · BUFFALO, NEW YORK

First Edition
Library of Congress Control Number: 2002101087
ISBN: 1-893996-51-4
Edited by Robert Alexander
Cover design by Percolator
Printed and bound in the United States of America
The Marie Alexander Poetry Series, number 5

The publication of *Moments Without Names* has been made possible by support
from Robert Alexander and with public funds from the New York State Council
on the Arts, a State Agency.

Cover illustration: "Symbolic Depiction of the Breach with the Medieval World
View," 1888. Wood engraving by an unknown artist, used with permission of
AKG Berlin/Superstock, Inc.

White Pine Press
P.O. Box 236
Buffalo, NY 14201

www.whitepine.org

ACKNOWLEDGMENTS:

The author wishes to thank the editors of the following publications, where most of the new poems first appeared, many of them in slightly different forms:

Alembic: "Words Before Sleep"

The Barnabe Mt. Review: "Memory," "Now," "Invitation to the Metaphysician's Cottage," "Spring Laughter"

The Bloomsbury Review: "The Lost Month"

Caesura: "Angels," "Waking"

Calapooya: "I Could Hear the Shouting"

Caliban: "Broken Symmetries"

Central Coast Review: "The Library"

Denver Quarterly: "Elegy for Things to Come," "Into the New Millennium" (as "Millennium's End"), "Fire," "Footnotes," "The Bread of My Life"

Durak: "The Moment for Which There is No Name"

Good Times: "Goodbye to the 20th Century"

Hanging Loose: "What's in a Name," "Hand Gestures," "Blinking," "Visions," "The Eternal Mystery is as Mysterious..."

Key Satch(el): "Departure"

Luna: "I Find the Letter," "Languedoc," "Flypaper," "The Boots in My Uncle's Closet"

Paragraph: "What Narcissus Saw," "The New Narcissus"

Ploughshares: "Incident From the Day of the Dead"

Poetry International: "Heart Attack"

Portland Review: "Moments I Cherish," "The Distant People"

The Prose Poem: An International Journal: "Three Heroes"

Quarry West: "Not Yet," "A Votive Offering to Sor Juana Inès de la Cruz"

Untitled: A Magazine of Prose Poetry: "The Photo of Pessoa's Trunk"

Almost a third of these poems originally appeared in the books The Armies Encamped in the Fields Beyond the Unfinished Avenues (Jazz Press, 1977) and When People Could Fly (Hanging Loose Press, 1997).

"The Library" originally appeared as a poster issued by the Friends of the Santa Cruz Libraries to celebrate National Library Week (1999).

I wish to give special thanks to Robert Alexander for his inspired and inspiring editing of this book, to Deng Ming-Dao for his many kindnesses and provocative comments and questions about the manuscript as it took shape, and to Hanging Loose Press for their generosity in releasing for this publication a good portion of When People Could Fly, which is still in print and should be considered a companion volume to this book.

*this book
is for you,
the reader*

BEGINNINGS

Broken Symmetries / 19
The Big Broadcast / 20
The Oceans / 21
The Stone Flowers / 23
The Lost Month / 24
The Duke, the Demon, and the Sacred Grove / 26
The Sorcerer's Apprentice / 28
The True Cross / 31
The Sorrow of Wood / 32
Three Lost Tales of the Baal Shem Tov / 33
Scenes From The Life of the Wandering Jew / 36
The Way of Our Fathers / 40
A Game of Chess / 42
The Words / 44
A Votive Offering To Sor Juana / 45
The Kiss / 47
The Mussorgsky Question / 49
Three Heroes / 52
The People of The Boat / 53
Now / 55
Culture / 56
Fire / 57

AT HOME

The Boots in My Uncle's Closet / 65
The Girl Who Became My Grandmother / 66
Waking / 68
What's in a Name / 69
The Bread of My Life / 70
My Father's Hobby / 71
A Treatise on Time / 72
The Head / 74
Blackboards / 77
Kisses / 78
The Dance / 80
What Fathers Do / 82
Monsters / 83
Discord / 84
Calendar / 85
Angel Incident / 86
"I Find the Letter" / 87
Moments Without Names / 88
Smoking Cigars / 90
Flypaper / 91
The Request / 93
The Story That Had Never Been Written / 95

ON STREETS & ROADS

Spring Laughter / 101
Friday, the 13th / 102
Departure / 103
In Passing / 104
Angels / 104
The Seduction of the Trees / 105
Gorilla / 106
Time & Again / 107
The Letter / 108
Hand Gestures / 109
How I Came to Own the World / 112
The Myth of History / 114
What Narcissus Saw / 116
The New Narcissus / 116
Visions / 117
Saints / 119
The Answer / 120
The Trick / 122
Waitresses / 123
The Ultimate Place of Exile / 125
The Distant People / 127
Men Who Cry / 129

TRAVELS

Journeys / 133
Tourists / 134
In the City of Sunlight / 135
The Cult of the Burning Flowers / 138
Languedoc / 140
The Exhibitionist / 141
Swallows / 143
The Face / 144
My Encounter With The Eternal Mystery / 145
Step on a Crack / 147
Invitation To The Metaphysician's Cottage / 149
The Bell at the Bottom of the Sea / 153
Vacation / 155
The 8th, 9th, and 10th Wonders of the World / 156
The Tale of a Doorknob / 158
Tears / 159
The Armies Encamped in the Fields / 160
"I Could Hear the Shouting" / 162
Doing It to Others / 164
Memory / 165
The Storyteller / 167
Moon & Flower / 170

ENDINGS

Goodbye to the Twentieth Century / 175
Into the New Millennium / 177
The Light Was Out / 178
"The Eternal Mystery is as Mysterious..." / 180
The Final Extinction / 181
Moments I Cherish / 182
The Photo of Pessoa's Trunk / 183
Reading George Seferis / 184
Backbone / 186
"Not Yet" / 188
Who Says We're Not Lucky? / 190
Heart Attack / 191
Footnotes / 192
The Moment for Which There is No Name / 194
Elegy for Things to Come / 195
Another Bite from the Cosmic Apple / 197
Blinking / 199
The Field / 200
At Peace / 201
Words Before Sleep / 202
Incident From the Day of the Dead / 203
The Library / 206

...These are my fancies, by which I try to give knowledge not of things, but of myself....As my fancies present themselves, I pile them up; now they come pressing in a crowd, now dragging single file. I want people to see my natural and ordinary pace, however off the track it is. I let myself go as I am....I seek only the learning that treats of the knowledge of myself and instructs me how to die well and live well....

—Michel de Montaigne

...I write to go through myself again and again....That is the adventure of being alive.

—Henri Michaux

...I place my hopes on a phantasmagoric art with hypotheses instead of purpose and grotesque instead of realistic descriptions of everyday life. It would correspond more fully to the spirit of our times. Let the fantastic images of Hoffmann, Dostoyevsky, Goya...and of many other realists and nonrealists teach us how to be truthful with the help of absurd fantasy.

—Abram Tertz
(Andrei Sinyavsky)

BEGINNINGS

"We live in a crystallized universe of broken symmetries," someone said, as if God in a rage had smashed all the chandeliers in His palace and left us to find our way in the dark.

That is why we wander here below in the afterlight of splintered glass strewn on the surface of what He remembers and we never knew.

The Big Broadcast

The universe lacks clarity. The edges of things scatter, explosions of light reaching out in sparks, filaments, threads that fray into the future of something else.

Knowledge is sequence, not tense, and in that sense space, not time, is ticking in our heads, matter is all that matters and nothing is the matter with that.

What is immortal in us is not moral but those feelers of light merging with the next object we touch, those antennae surrounding us like radiant body hairs that sip from something else which will, in turn, sip from us whatever, at that instant, we are.

The sound of the universe is not static, but sucking and slurping, each form passing on the message that needs no decoding because it is encoded in every thing: you eat me and I eat you, a light meal arriving from the kitchen of the sun.

The radio signals from deep space broadcast soap operas, *crimes passionels*, injustices, private and public scandals more (or less) lurid than those we devise because they are us:

She loved him and he did or did not love her, God's radiant lips appearing out of the eternal dark to thunder against each other like a celestial radio announcer's, telling us to tune in, not out, same time, same place, because the universe, more quarky than quirky, will be continued.

THE OCEANS

Don't remind me that we resemble the seas, that we are 67% water, and that the taste of our tears is salt from the ocean deeps.

I want to forget those vast uncertainties that go on doing what they do each day, year after year, unable to find any peace.

Their restlessness unnerves me. Their frustrated rages incite my own, as they shift one way and another, shaking their fists at the stars, going nowhere, stuck to the depressions of the planet from which they cannot escape.

And yet I do not look forward to the day when the oceans will rise up and wrench themselves free, dragging all our memories with them.

In a dream once I saw the oceans surging and tumbling through space, stretching and contracting into any shape they could imagine, sporting like a school of dolphin, as they experienced for the first time the joy of being whatever they wanted to be.

In their excitement, however, they forgot where they were, and looking over their shoulders they searched for that cinder which for eons they had considered, for want of a better name, home.

But the cinder was no longer there. At the oceans' departure, it had continued spinning in the opposite direction, so the location the oceans sought was a calculation that pinpointed empty space.

Now the oceans existed in an endless moment, a continuous vacancy that extended in all directions, and it made no difference where they moved or how they moved there.

Soon they began to founder and roll, tentatively feeling with their edges for any kind of landfall.

Finally, they were shapeless masses, without sound or meaning, unable to cry out the immense longings they contained for imprisoning shorelines and lost tides.

THE STONE FLOWERS

for Donna

There was a time when stones flowered. I need to believe that. In forests and fields, layers of black rock cracked open after rain, and slick pink petals swarmed into the wet sunlight. And those who saw this weren't astonished because such blossomings happened all the time.

As recently as the nineteenth century, miners reported seeing chunks of coal blossom with blue flowers as tenuous as flames. Some said walls of coal sprouted blue flowers all around them, and with picks at their sides they stood speechless at the wonder of it.

On the beach at night, I've seen the sand shimmer with a green phosphorescence. The next day I imagined the sand was acres of seeds, and I thought, "That's what this Earth is: seeds."

And when I look up at the stars sometimes, I think that's what this planet is, a seed hurtling with others through space.

When my wife weeps for our son or the death of a relative, I think of all the seeds—scattered over the earth like unlit points of light—lying gray and dull next to golden specks of mica and the glassed-in worlds of opal with their trapped swirls of celestial flame.

I know that the earth is full of cinders and hard seeds that have never blossomed, and that it makes no difference if pink flowers once surged from layers of black rock, or if one day the planet will crack open and shoot a pink and blue geyser into the night that will unfurl like a celestial flower.

I know that whether times are good or bad, we ride this planet like mites crawling on a pebble.

That is why I am not ashamed to say that flowers once blossomed from stone: I need to believe in every possibility. We all do.

THE LOST MONTH

There was a month that got lost among the other months, much as a child is lost in a forest at nightfall and wanders through the darkness, unable to find its way home.

How such an event could have happened has never been explained. One theory contends that much as a chapter can fall from a poorly bound book, scattering its pages everywhere, the month fell from the year, strewing its days in such hopeless disarray that they were unable to find their way back not only to their previous order within the month, but to the month itself. The month, meanwhile, no longer containing any days, disappeared, and its days remained randomly dispersed among the other months all the way down to the present.

In such a theory, it is not difficult to identify the days of the lost month from other days. They are the unhappy ones—the days when a parent dies, workers lose jobs, wars are declared, or people are raped and murdered: those days when bitterness or despair move us to commit acts against neighbors and animals and trees that shock us in their cruelty, and we say it was the wind, the heat of the sun, something about that particular day that drove us to it, as if the day itself were responsible for our behavior.

Astronomers say this talk of a lost month is nonsense: that, true, the months are longer or shorter on calendars of different civilizations, but the reasons for such fluctuations have to do with mathematical accuracy, usually involving the length of the earth's annual trip around the sun. They even acknowledge that the Sumerian calendar had a floating month that would appear out of nowhere every several years, and that an early Roman calendar was only ten months long.

Certainly, therefore, the possibility of a month erased from all our calendars is not farfetched—a lost month like a tribe cursed out of a holy land, one that even when we mention it causes us to cross ourselves, or bite our lips, or hold our children close: a tribe that practiced acts of incest and torture and self-mutilation, but whose members in face and form are indistinguishable from us, and who over the eons have infiltrated all societies, intermarried and bred offspring with tendencies as dark and devious as their own, off-spring who do not know why they do what they do, or when they will do it, except that their anomalous behavior is dictated by "bad days" or "phases of the moon."

Another theory maintains that the lost month was banished from calendars because it was the 13th month, and in ancient times priests and scholars distributed its unlucky days judiciously among the other months, but over the millennia, which have become more and more crowded with the rubble of fallen empires and their calendars, the locations of those days have been forgotten, so that now we must remain anxious and terrified from one day to the next, not knowing what to expect, as if each of us was a child lost in a windy forest at nightfall every evening of the year.

THE DUKE, THE DEMON AND THE SACRED GROVE

for George Ow, Jr.

The duke of Jin dreamt that a demon with hair of fire and lumpy, boil-strewn skin smashed through the palace gates and the doors of the inner apartments and stood at the foot of his bed, howling for vengeance.

"What does this mean?" the duke asked the sorcerer of the Bamboo Grove the next morning.

"Your highness will not live to eat the new grain," the old man replied.

Three months later, the duke summoned the sorcerer to attend him at a banquet, a ceremonial occasion featuring buns made from the grain the duke had levied as taxes on the latest harvest. "Your error has cost you your life," he said to the old man, nodding to a guard, who decapitated the sorcerer on the spot.

No sooner had the duke swallowed the first bun, however, than his stomach swelled from the grain and he fell dead.

The story concludes with a middle-aged servant who the night before, huddling in a stable and shivering from cold, had dreamt that he was carrying the duke to heaven on his back. Because of this dream, he is the one ordered to haul the duke's body from the banquet table to the mortuary, and is then beheaded so his spirit can accompany the duke's on its heavenly journey.

I always confuse this story with another from the same book. In the second tale, a brash young man challenges the Sacred Grove to a game of dice, wagering his life against the use of the Grove's resident genie. He tosses the dice for the Grove and himself and wins, but the Grove, which has said nothing to the young man from the start, will not give up its Spirit and, despite this ecologically symbolic stance, rots and dies within the week.

My confusion begins when I look up the second story in the book, *The Zou Zhuan And Other Classics of Early Chinese History*, and find that the tale I remembered is not the one there. It turns out that for some unknown reason the Grove has consented to the wager, lends its Spirit to the young man as agreed, but dies because the young man refuses to return the Spirit at the appointed time.

This version is certainly more plausible and ecologically suggestive than mine, but within a day I am again confusing the story in the book with the one I imagined. Add to this the notion I got from heaven knows where that the demon of the duke's dream is really the Spirit of the Sacred Grove gone berserk because he could no longer find his home, that the sorcerer of the Bamboo Grove is the brash young man grown old, and that the grain which swells the duke's stomach is a seed that contains the beginnings of a new Sacred Grove but was snatched from the genie's hand as he was about to plant it—and it is clear that somewhere in my psyche the genie howls vengeance at the foot of the duke's bed because he envisions the duke three months later devouring the future he has been robbed of in the past.

I guess joining the two tales together and extrapolating from them fulfills a need in me that insists on creating order from chaos, so that my confusing the stories, in the end, is a way of making everything clear. Everything, that is, except the servant who dreamt the wrong dream at the wrong time. Unless, of course, poor, in rags, needing to pay a compulsory state tax he could not afford, the servant is the one who snatched the seed from the genie's hand as he was about to plant it.

Tiresias is sitting in the doorway of his hut, his skirts hiked up showing his withered inner thighs, as he stares at the town below with sightless eyes.

He has just been told by his page, the boy who leads him, who cooks for him and washes his clothes, who bathes and oils his wrinkled reptilian skin, that the queen is dead and the young king, after stabbing out his eyes, has been led away in misery and ruin; that everything he told the king two hours before has come to pass.

The old man shuffles his sandals in the dust. The boy sees no pleasure in his face. The quarrelsome prophet, whose feisty frame shook with anger at the king a short time before, does not look satisfied. Like the universe, he is expressionless and blind.

Bending forward on his golden staff, the old man looks as if he's peering into the future, but the boy knows that posture is only the way the old rise or remain steady even when they sit, leaning their weight on anything that will hold them up.

If the old man sees anything, the boy thinks, it is the last thing he ever saw. Out hunting on Helicon as a youth no older than the boy is now, he came thirsty to the spring around a hill, and found the goddess naked, bathing there, her body so dazzling its reflection was sunlight glancing off the water and shattering like glass in both his eyes.

That was not her punishment, but the Law's: to see the unseeable, the boy knows, is to lose one's sight. In compensation, the goddess gave the old man inner vision, declaring him prophet with the power to speak with birds, and handed him the staff he leans on now to guide him through his darkened days.

What the boy cannot perceive is what the old man thinks; that knowing is the curse that gives the prophet such little pleasure he can no longer force a single expression to flutter across his bony face.

The prophet knew Oedipus's fate years ago, saw behind his clouded eyes the queen, Oedipus's wife and mother, swinging in a noose above her bed even before the child was born. In the same way, he sees himself years from now in the land of the dead, enticed through dim caverns to drink from the pit of blood Odysseus will prepare in order to learn from him the way home.

The way home. Why is it always that and not the other, more pertinent question: whether the life at home will warrant the hardships of the journey. Home for Oedipus was horror, was husbanding his mother and murdering his father. It is the place from which he has been driven now, a wanderer once again, knowing but sightless, cursed as he, the aged prophet, all these years has been. The boredom Odysseus will find at home will be no better.

The old man sits back, letting the staff fall against his shoulder like the great oar he will tell Odysseus to bring into the land where men are ignorant of the sea. Useless advice, always useless: to know the future but to be unable to change it. That's the knowledge that sears his inner sight, just as his vision of the goddess had scorched his eyeballs and burned his optic nerves like candlewicks.

The boy knows none of this. He watches the old man lift the staff from his shoulder with both hands and, as he has done so many times before, tease the dust before him with its tip. Sometimes the prophet absently sketches pictures in the dust, or traces words whose esoteric meanings only the birds can understand, and his face, expressionless as always, will be lost somewhere beyond his body and the world.

At such times, the boy who leads him, who cooks for him and washes his clothes, who bathes and rubs his reptilian skin with fragrant oils, watches fascinated, silently moving his lips as he memorizes the words and imitates the old man's drawings with a slen-

der twig, scratching in the dirt those symbols he doesn't compre-
hend. Once he scrapes the twig against the ground, he is unable to
stop, although he is shaken with nausea and becomes deliriously
ill, while the stick—he's sworn to several friends—trembles in his
hand like a snake about to awaken from a trance.

THE TRUE CROSS

for Clem Starck

We never ask if, as carpenter, he thought about the proportions and notched connections, or how well the wood was planed and the pieces fit, when he first grasped the rough cross. Remember, he had the trained eye, the professional's ability to estimate shoddy work or work well done. Did he, for a moment, want to redo or improve that instrument of his death?

I ask this in all seriousness. The True Cross scraped against his fingertips and palms, maybe catching on calluses and cuts, maybe resting on the grooved lifeline that was about to run out, and I imagine he must have been more engrossed by those shreds of experience than any notions of resurrection or everlasting life.

The iron nails that slammed through his palms and attached him to the wood, glancing off bone and shattering knuckles, had to be large enough to support the weight of a man, let alone a god. Did he appreciate the bureaucratic thoroughness that had taken into consideration even that?

The man who built the True Cross must have risen before dawn in the chilly blue light, and maybe grumbled that he had to make three crosses before nine that morning. Possibly his wife called to him as he left the hut to remind him of their visit to her parents' house that evening, or to ask him for a few dinars to buy cloth that afternoon in the marketplace, where, she said, she planned to go, unless the crowds were too large because of the executions announced for later in the day.

THE SORROW OF WOOD

It is recorded that on his travels Rabbi Nachman of Bratzlav was unable to sleep one night when he stayed in a cabin made of new logs. He was kept awake by moanings everywhere around him, which none of his companions could hear. "It was the pain of the trees that had been cut down to build the house," he explained the next day. "Their grief surrounded me and I could not rest."

The Rabbi was moved by the sorrow of wood, a sorrow that ascends like sap through the trees, as it does through us, drawn upward from the earth until it returns to the light from the highest leaves.

For what has died and gone back into the earth rises through us and lives again. We are nourished from below by hidden springs that drain through the stones with endless wailings that few of us can hear, but through those laments we flourish and dance in the sunlit wind before we return as water to the buried stones.

Three Lost Tales of the Baal Shem Tov

Who has not heard of the Baal Shem Tov? Each of his tales is a leaf on the tree of his legend, the tree that shines like a shaft of flame in the shadowy garden of our imagination.

*

"Forget about how many angels dance on the point of a pin, or how many souls can slide through the eye of a needle. Those problems are the syllogisms of tailors," he said. "The only question worth asking is whether the dead push us from the earth through the tree, so they can fly once more from the wings of the leaves, or whether we're dragged upwards from the stones until like birds we sing the praises of God from the highest branches."

When asked in Berditchev whether he thought we were shoved from below or tugged from above, he answered, "From above. It's God's way of glorifying the dead."

Another time, in Kamenetz, he answered, "From below. It's the dead's way of glorifying us."

However, in Horodenko he replied to a feeble old man leaning on his grandson, "Both. It's God's way of glorifying the dead and their way of glorifying us."

But when he was asked this same question in Sadigor by a drayman whose wife had recently died, he said, "Neither. What makes you think our lives are dependent on the whims of God or the dead and have nothing to do with us?"

"How can this be!" cried Reb Tzvi-Hersh Sofier, the Baal Shem's lifelong scribe, as the crowd in the Sadigor marketplace stood astonished. "Two years ago you answered, 'From above.' Last year, 'From below.' Two months ago, 'Both.' And now, 'None of the three.'"

The Baal Shem turned to his scribe, nodded toward the drayman's sad eyes and dishevelled clothes, and said, shaking his head, "Tzvi, Tzvi!"

Later that day when they were walking alone on the road to Polnoye, the frustrated scribe trotted around his master and continued to upbraid him. "How could you say that God determines our lives in one place, that the dead do in another, that both do in a third, and that we do in a fourth?"

The master shrugged. "Tzvi, you never look to see whom I am talking to. For each of the four there was a correct answer that wasn't correct for the others. Besides, I'm sure you think that at least one of the answers was right, so why quibble?"

*

Clapping his hands, a disciple of the Baal Shem leaped up from the prayer table, beaming. "I've just discovered men and women's most important secret: they love God, whether they know it or not."

The Baal Shem looked up from a letter he had just received, and nodded. "Good. Now you have to learn God's most important secret with equal conviction."

"What's that?" asked the disciple.

"Why," said the Baal Shem turning back to the letter, "that whether or not God knows it, He loves us."

*

This is what the Baal Shem Tov, the Master of the Holy Name, said to his disciples as they rested in a forest on the road to Lwow:

"I have told you how enraptured I was when I was alone in the mountains. I learned the language of stones and trees, of donkeys and sparrows, and I have told you how hard it was to come down into the towns and villages and live among people.

34

"But I have also told you that we *must* live among people, with their sorrows and pettiness, their transgressions and self-righteousness, no matter how much we yearn to remain with the wind of God's voice on the mountain tops.

"To live with people and help them is our duty. But we also have a duty to go into the mountains so we never lose touch with God's voice.

"Many of you have said that these two roles are a contradiction. But are they? There is the raindrop we see that taps the surface of the pond and makes the water shudder in all directions. That is our life among people and shows how each of our actions affects others.

"However, there is the raindrop we don't see that slips through the surface and disappears without a ripple, as if the surface had opened a tiny fish mouth, closed around the raindrop like a pearl, and swallowed it without leaving a trace. This is our life alone.

"Who is to say which raindrop is doing God's work and which is not? Both are part of a community of raindrops that are collectively called a pond, which at night luminously reflects the stars, many of which we recognize and many we do not, and some we do not even notice as they slide down the sky and disappear."

SCENES FROM THE LIFE OF THE WANDERING JEW

1. The First Return
The port opens its silver waters. A foghorn drones.

He stands on the lower deck, staring through the stippled half-light, the gray hush, to the barely visible houses packed along the quay.

No one is there to meet him. Has he returned for this?

The keys sharpen their teeth in his pocket. His passport and papers flare in the suitcase at his side. Somewhere in the city, a house turns toward the water, like an old elephant with tired eyes. The gypsies are parading on the boulevards. He can hear the tambourines shivering above the crowd, the fiddle music sliding down side streets to the pier.

The ship bumps against the dock, the gangplank falls. He descends with his suitcase.

There is no one about, and the ship recedes behind him like an iceberg.

As in the other cities, he has only his footsteps—only his footsteps to carry him through the deserted streets toward the familiar voices, which, he now realizes, he can hardly recognize.

2. Other Returns
His marriages were annulled by rivers.

When he crossed each one and looked back, each of his wives was disappearing into the mist, her hand stretched toward him.

Each morning the sun unscrolled the scriptures of saints on the landscape. He watched. He read promises and prophecies, and his mouth repeated them until his words quivered like daggers in the ground, until the rivers were leaping tongues of acid and the landscape was covered with broken dishes.

What did the others know, with their encyclopedias and altars? His glory was founded on an error, and he trudged in its light the rest of his days, knowing a wife or a war was a place one left behind, and that all the riches of this world tumbled down the ravines of one's sorrows.

Each night, huddled inside his shadow, he would mumble into the huge darkness.

When he returned, everyone knew him. They pointed and called. Some cheered. All pushed his wife toward him, but she held back when she saw his eyes.

They were strangers, all of them. They meant nothing to him. And once more he turned toward the city gates.

3. On The Road
He met others along the way.

Like routed armies, they staggered past him, sometimes asking for directions, sometimes for bread.

These were the people he recognized: horsemen without horses, farmers without farms, workers without work. Men and women both. They all fell to their knees, ripping at weeds and dust which they brought to their mouths, hissing and growling.

He had fallen himself, more than once, felt the light tilt in his eyes like ground glass, uttered the same noises.

What on this earth is sacred to those who have been denied sanctity? Not desire, not the pursuit of one's desires, not even all the radiant griefs of the world held in one's arms, but only those words simply uttered in a trembling voice: "Stranger, stay for a moment, stay."

4. The Griefs

The griefs visited him one by one.

They swayed around him, a dance of suppliant kings. A sorrow, a fever, a cancerous noise munching sloppily on silence.

The old, the young, swayed with them, an endless line that moved over hills and out of sight.

But he stood apart. He defied ambition and grief. And when he returned to the city for the thousandth time, all we recognized of him was this gesture of defiance, a gesture we had made ourselves once or twice in order to survive, and had then forgotten.

But this gesture was all he was now, and recognizing this may have made him a martyr to us but never a saint.

He tramped through the crowds, seeing no one.

5. The Final Day

"It was the hour the stars stopped in their courses and glittered their serpent eyes down through the dark.

"It was the hour of the sailors' return, when the ancient ships, rotting boards and seaweed, reared like horses from the waves.

"And then all the world's coffins sailed toward me and flowed past, that great fleet without sails or sickness.

"The fragments of history rose to their knees, trembling.

"Blind, flaking parchment, grandmothers and grandfathers began their stuttering steps.

"What could I say, even now a stranger, who turned with the others toward that final day?

"What could I say of the laughter, the sorrows, now heaped with nervous rats on the eons of devoured meals that steamed on rickety tables?

"It was the hour the decrepit mendicants had been dragging toward all their years.

"I saw a chair beneath a tree. Apples and plums were dropping around it, but no one stopped to eat.

"It was the hour when memory became vanity or was called for in vain and it didn't matter which one, the hour when all the words flew out of books and all the songs gave up their melodies.

"I stumbled among feathers and bones that fluttered and took wing.

"It was neither winter nor summer, but a time when shadows were luminous and all the alleys were passages of light.

"When my name was called, I didn't answer. Everything was silent, still. A wind was scratching in an empty bowl.

"For the last time, I turned toward the light that was no longer light, to the day that was no longer day.

"But when my name was called again, I could not bring myself to turn back."

THE WAY OF OUR FATHERS

for Geoffrey Dunn

Arctic angels hurl diagonals of light from the clouds. Icebergs fall as we pass. In the distance, whales and sea serpents are scroll-work on a pewter sea, as the gods tumble and wrestle overhead.

We continually turn to each other without speaking, our eyes filled with terror as much as wonder, our beards and furs bristling with cobwebs that shatter when we brush them away.

Where is he taking us? Is he still in command, or is a lodestone under the keel hauling us to an inglorious end?

We signed on because it was spring and the way of our fathers. Yawning and stretching, we jostled one another as we clambered aboard, and he pushed off before most of us had set our oars in their grooves or warmed the benches.

Now this. We wanted the squirming women of the south, their scent of warm milk and damp grasses, the thatched villages shivering into shreds from our axes, or exploding into flame. That was the way of our fathers. "Give us that," we said. "Where are you taking us?"

"This is the way of our fathers," he replied: "to learn new ways, to discover new lands." And at first we accepted his words, remembering his legendary luck. To hell with that! Rather talk about *his* father's ways—murderer and outcast. Rather talk about the curse than the luck.

The way of our fathers is to plunder the south, as the way of our mothers is to mourn us when we do not return, and to praise us when we do, their eyes fixed on our armloads of jewels and richly embroidered clothes.

Follow him? Where? Why? Doesn't he feel the cold deepening more every hour, the stillness expanding around us in all directions?

At any moment the sea will harden into acres of ice and we will be marooned here like the whales and the serpents—figures on a silver bell whose tolling will be the only explanation for our presence on this eternal sea.

A Game of Chess

I have recently read that Hernando De Soto, captain in Charles V's expeditionary forces in the New World, taught the most high Inca chieftain Atahualpa to play chess during the chieftain's imprisonment in 1532, those uncertain months before the cutthroat Pizarro decided it would be best if Atahualpa were dead, because the body of a nation without its head....

I looked up from the book and wondered whose life such information changes. Mine? Yours? No one's—except, of course, Atahualpa's and, in a different way, Pizarro's and De Soto's?

I had learned as a boy that De Soto discovered the Mississippi River in 1541 and died exploring it, his body in its armor heaved into the river, where it sank like a cannon ball, while his men, alone and terrified in the wilderness, wept.

In 1946 my uncle, who would fail in ten businesses and end his days as a gentle orderly in the Long Island Hospital for the Insane, drove a two-door forest-green sedan called a De Soto, and while sitting in the passenger seat next to him I'd stare for what seemed hours at the center of the steering wheel, where a medallion depicted the profile of the old conquistador with pointed beard and Spanish helmet. The medallion was colored gold and looked like a coin lying on a circular bed of crimson silk.

Years later, when I lived near the Mississippi, I remembered the shadowy interior of my uncle's car and his childlike laughter as he steered us north and south on our expeditions through the wilds of Brooklyn for a bottle of milk. His hands, displaying the only confidence he ever had, gripped the steering wheel where the medallion glowed like a saint's medal within the circle of his arms.

And when I walked along the Mississippi's banks, the brown water sliding by me, I would picture the muddy current like a drowned wind dragging through De Soto's upturned rib cage. Half sunk in the silt beside it, the rusted remains of arquebuses, swords, and armor every so often released a particle of rusted metal to the current as it sped southward, twisting and turning and tumbling the particle end over end with the bone flakes of Ojibwas and Dakotas, carrying them with uprooted tree trunks and bloated cows all the way to the Gulf of Mexico.

Now I follow those waters fanning out in the Gulf, cross Mexico and work my way south along the Andes to a side room in the stone fortress of Cajamarca where De Soto sits across a chessboard from Atahualpa. Hernando is holding up the knight on horseback with one hand and pointing to it with the other, and saying in exaggerated Spanish, "He arrives on horseback, prancing two steps to the side and one step forward. He never comes straight at you. So beware."

Which one is it then—Atahualpa reaching for the piece, or Hernando holding it from him—who a moment later laughs my uncle's childlike laugh.

The Words

When we sleep, the words inside us slide from their hiding places like thieves and assassins in a Renaissance city.

It is after midnight, but there are all these figures, muffled in cloaks or slipping from one pillar to another in black capes, who whisper and bicker, or come upon one another unexpectedly in the dark.

One stabs another in a shadowy arcade, and leaves the body where it falls. At the edge of a piazza, four ruffians, growling and cursing, carry off a drunken student in a burlap sack.

The façades of townhouses are still and dark, although whimpers and sighs and raspy snores flutter from the partially open windows, their meanings blurred by the fountains burbling in the squares.

The quiet everywhere is stippled by these sounds, as if the buildings were restless and muttering.

A shout. Lights flare at windows. Torches dot a piazza. It seems the body has been found.

But the sounds are confused, the reports garbled. Is it war, disease, the birth of an heir in the prince's palace?

A bell booms in a cathedral tower. The sound rushes in all directions over the tile rooftops.

A mile or two down the road leading to the city's west gate, a peasant in a cart lets his donkey guide him home as he sings of love, death, and the joys of a simple life.

A Votive Offering
to Sor Juana Inès de la Cruz

Sor Juana, whenever I try to picture your life, I wonder what daily sounds jangled the air around your hood: not the distant noises from a walled-out Mexico City circa 1688, but the more immediate sounds you heard as you strode through the convent's covered walkways. And I wonder if you listened for a particular sound, one that would unify all the others, arrange the random noises of your day into a meaningful system, a catalogue that made sense of such trivia as the scraping sandals on the tiles, the rustling of starched Carmelite cowls, the *chink-chink* of rosaries bobbing on the other sisters' outer garments, while their bodies, like currents below ocean swells, rolled beneath layers of robes and scratchy underclothes.

Was that sound always just out of reach, always beyond your grasp—whispers from another cell, murmurs in the corridor, the continuous echoes and closing doors like faraway thunder in distant halls?

And the shadows swishing around corners and down unlit passageways: did you wonder who would emerge from them, hands clasped together, floating and dipping in nun's apparel, as if whoever appeared entered from another world?

That was it: you were always confronting the life beyond this one, like the cries and drunken voices bickering and calling beyond the convent walls. You were always trying to discover how this world and the other one fit: how your stumbling heart was part of the body around it, and your body part of the enclosing robes, just as you wondered how the convent fit into the encircling city, and the city into the surrounding countryside with its new churches and toppled Aztec ruins, its Spanish and Indian populace. All were different yet the same, separate yet somehow one: circles within circles that did not touch, like the celestial spheres you were told kept their separate orbits in the orderly universe that revolved above your head.

This is the world you knew yet did not know, the life you led but did not lead, its lack of connections driving you to books and scientific experiments, so you would be able to see what could not be seen, the invisible way things intersect and merge.

And so it was that one night you dreamed, and in your dream rose above the convent and the city, streamed skyward above the continent and the moon-flecked oceans on either side of your narrow land. You slid upward, propelled by your passion for knowing, the sounds of the planet not receding behind you but hauled up in your wake—the babbling and laughter, the bleating and silent screams.

And what you found, hovering in space, was not Ptolemy's circles within circles, not shining concentric rings, but the center of a single circle, and that center was everywhere: a circle without circumference, like the mouth of a barrel without sides, an emptiness containing all things—animals, vegetables, stones—and each performed in relation to the others to create a harmonious whole.

It was a vision that could be glimpsed but not held, intuited but not comprehended. But as always, you wanted complete comprehension, and so for you the mystic center would not stay, and you fell through the night, and the dream fell with you, fell back into your body, as pieces of our dreams fall back into ours like specks of moonlight showering the darkened city states of our cells. And when you woke, you woke in the convent of your body, as we wake each morning isolated from the rioting world beyond the body's walls.

It was your first dream, and your last. The second dream is ours, who follow in your wake. The dream sleeps in us, just out of reach, as it did in you, a lit candle in our cloistered hearts. In bed at night, we can hear the candle fluttering deep inside, like a butterfly wing impatient to take flight. I can hear it now, this dream of unity that wants to be wakened in us all, and that was first envisioned in this hemisphere by you, a childless nun whose children we are.

THE KISS

Paris. July 7, 1792. The Revolution is about to collapse. For weeks the representatives, cursing and shouting, have scurried from group to group, or muttered behind each other's backs in the halls of the Assembly, unable to agree, it seems, on anything, as the food shortage continues and reports of invading armies, plots and counterplots, increase in number and wildness every hour.

Outside, crowds roam the streets, armed with pikes, pickaxes, and flintlocks spiked with fixed bayonets.

The representatives have taken to yelling and railing at one another in every session of the Assembly. They are doing so this morning as the Abbé Antoine Adrien Lamourette rises from his seat. He raises his right arm for silence from his 700 colleagues, some of whom are dozing, others reading newspapers, while the majority whisper feverishly or declaim in small groups.

"*Liberté*," he calls, and everyone turns to listen. "*Egaliteé, fraternité*," he says. "*L'amour*." Only love can save us, brotherly love. This is what the Revolution is all about and why we are here. We should pledge to hold this love as our first principle, he says, and seal the vow with a kiss.

For a moment no one moves. Then all at once the representatives, enemies and friends, are cheering, throwing hats in the air, embracing one another, kissing and laughing, as tears course down their faces.

It is only a gesture, of course. Within the hour, they will be bickering and arguing again, and within two months the Paris mob will supplant the debates with the rising of August 10th and the September Massacres.

To me, however, Lamourette and his proposal, and the Assembly's spontaneous reaction to it, is a reminder. When I'm most in despair at the hatreds and brutalities of my fellow humans, I think of him and his kiss, and I imagine that some kind of natural order, neither moral or religious, is at work in us—a twitch in our cells, a speck in our chromosomes—that tries to guide us back on course; and that even in the most tumultous human interactions it makes itself known.

Could the Abbé's name really be a coincidence? Lamourette. In English it means "a little love."

THE MUSSORGSKY QUESTION

The Mussorgsky question is an intriguing one: Should he be taken seriously as a composer, or was he merely a talented dilettante? Balakirev said, "His brains are weak." Tchaikovsky considered him to be talented but concluded that "he has a narrow stature and lacks the need for self-perfection." Tolstoy dismissed him by saying, "I like neither talented drunks nor drunken talents!"

A heavyset man with a clown's red nose and eyes that seemed circled by charcoal, Mussorgsky was drunk much of the time and at the end lived in a single room strewn with plates of half-eaten food and empty vodka bottles.

No one knew, however, that Mussorgsky was Dostoyevsky's greatest creation. So great, he sprang from the novelist's pen full-grown— and very drunk—on a stormy night in 1839, when Dostoyevsky, dreaming of becoming a writer, was an eighteen-year-old student at the school of Military Engineering.

Yet over the next forty-one years, the author didn't know where to place Mussorgsky: he was too talented to play Sonya's father or any of the other drunks who stumble through the pages of Dostoyevsky's novels.

Nevertheless, the author never abandoned the idea of using Mussorgsky, and put him on the Nevsky Prospekt until he found a suitable part for him in one of his books.

As drunks will, Mussorgsky wandered away, bewildered by all the lights and jingling horse-drawn sleighs. He vaguely remembered that he was a minor clerk in the Department of Forestry and a former officer in the Preobrajensky Guards, but he didn't know how he came to be shambling through the streets of St. Petersburg. Since he was a drunk, however, he went in search of the first tavern he could find to solve his confusion.

Like all Dostoyevsky characters, Mussorgsky was an idea sur-rounded by flesh and clothes, so single-minded and uncompro-mising, as ideas are, that he could never adjust to life. He had given up his army career to compose and lived only for music. Elegant, witty, perfumed and slim, he grew corpulent and shabby and would disappear for months on end, surfacing more disheveled and delirious than he had been before.

Periodically realizing that Mussorgsky was not where he had left him, Dostoyevsky would hunt him down and bring him home, making him wait in a straight back chair in front of his desk, while he sought a place for him in the novel he was currently writing. This would go on for weeks, Mussorgsky all the while sitting upright, licking his lips and looking moist-eyed around the room for bottles.

Other than physically, Mussorgsky was half-formed in every way, even in music, where his harmonies and structure were so "rough" and "wrong" they inspired Rimsky-Korsakov, Ravel and others to revise and rescore them in the forms we know them today, although how much of the music is theirs and how much is this bumbling phantom's, who may have existed only as an uncom-fortable but thrilling thought in their conventional minds, we will never know.

Dostoyevsky never used Mussorgsky. Those other drunks, Marmeladov and Snegyrov, were minor figures who functioned per-fectly as victims, sufferers at the hands of others. But Mussorgsky—Mussorgsky was special: he had the soul of an artist, and this Dostoyevsky did not know how to handle. Possibly Mussorgsky was closer to Dostoyevsky's character than the novelist dared to under-stand.

With the creation of Ilusha's alcoholic father in *The Brothers Karamazov*, Doystoyevsky stopped trying to find a niche in his books for the composer. Once again, he put Mussorgsky on the boulevard and, shoving him forward, he withdrew for the last time.

Mussorgsky was more bewildered than ever. How was a character supposed to behave who was created for a book that was never written? How was he to function? What was he to do? We can appreciate these questions, Dear Reader, since one way or another we ask them of ourselves almost every day.

In the end, Mussorgsky composed three operas and a handful of song cycles and tone poems. All are poorly written. No wonder many consider him a dabbler in music.

Composer or dilettante? Is that the Mussorgsky question? Or is it about the model who inspired others to be better than themselves by being so single-minded, so dedicated to his art that alcohol was the only other thing that had a place in his life? His commitment was so uncompromising that he could never be believable as a character in a novel, or for that matter as a human being.

The Brothers Karamazov was published in December, 1880. Dostoyevsky died of hemorrhaging lungs on January 28, 1881. Six weeks later, on March 16, Mussorgsky, enfeebled and suffering from delirium tremens for the previous two months, died of a stroke.

Both men are buried in the graveyard of the Alexander Nevsky Monastery.

THREE HEROES

1.

Zapata rode a white stallion. When it galloped, its tail and mane were clouds swirling into storms. And when it sauntered into a village plaza, everyone knew that the man in the saddle was no ordinary campesino: under the wide brim of his sombrero, the mud-brown eyes were of the earth, their earth, as if their anguish and anger and the sweat of their labor had taken the shape of a man who had come to avenge them all.

2.

The Baal Shem rode in a buggy tugged by a donkey. A big man with broad shoulders and ponderous belly, he was too large for the rig, but he rode in it over the rooftops of Eastern Europe, this tavern keeper touched by God, this confidant of angels, who was such a comforting thought in the minds of his people that when he clopped through a marketplace everyone nodded and smiled, so happy to know he was there that it made no difference whether he was on his way to wrestle the Evil One or to fill a grocery list.

3.

Sor Juana Inès de la Cruz slid through the covered walkways and sacred portals of old Mexico, the black hood tenting her head in the same way the black habit tented her body, as if she moved through a longitude of night containing continents and oceans. It was a night where plunging ships wrenched the knowledge of the past into the future and where, here and there in darkened villages, specks of light, fluttering from the windows of earthen huts, identified solitary figures reading at candlelit tables, learning from the great books of the dead how to make life better for the living.

The People of the Boat

I.

Watching the shaggy shoreline separate into rocks and trees, we experienced a moment of questioning as well as foreboding: Had we been driven here by exile or loss—the remnants of a ragged army in defeat; or had we undertaken the journey like a choir whose singing was a splendor that drove the ships in clouds of glory to this other world—this world that, one way or the other, offered a promise we had to believe in?

While we swung axes and sledge hammers, felled birch trees and pine, while we lashed logs into walls, tarred roofs and boiled tallow—these questions drove our days: why were we building, for what purpose—His glory or our own? And what, in the end, was the promise we expected to be fulfilled?

II.

The same questions were asked by those in the ships that followed, when they saw the jagged outlines of the cities we had built, although, admittedly, even for us these questions were rarely put into words. They were more a feeling—a foreboding.

And the forebodings grew, along with the ghosts of animals and painted people we had scrubbed from the land in the same way we scrubbed sweat from our bodies and noxious dreams from our minds—in the same way we erased the old customs and former languages from our memories.

III.

What had been promised? Had we sought freedom here, or had we been seduced by images of gold and goods, which make each of our cities look like a maze of marketplaces?

Had we sought escape in coming, remembering the armies at our back, or, as we told the young, had we chosen—faces forward in the salt wind—to seek a home where our ideas would take root in the landscape?

Or were both conceptions, in the end, one and the same?

IV.

Those who arrive now expect to see the cities on their horizons. Many have memorized the skylines and the famous buildings, and those who come with the old questions soon forget them in a tumult of forebodings.

Almost everyone thinks the cities were promised them, or they think nothing at all. The marketplace explains their days: the putting on equals the taking off, the spending is nearly as important as the getting, and "desiring" and "praying" are interchangeable in daily speech.

V.

The populace bustles through the streets, jostling those who wander among them wild-eyed and mumbling like shipwrecked sailors lost in a land whose ways they cannot comprehend.

Storms gather behind the buildings, cloudbanks that rumble like old forebodings. "It is weather, only weather," the people say. "It will vanish in a deluge of rain." But by this even the newcomers mean a new kind of rain, one that bites at the buildings and streets like teeth in the jaws of avenging ghosts.

Now

Now is when everything happens, that word I left behind at the beginning of this sentence, and move farther away from with each breath.

To get back to it is to become a historian, or a furniture mover in the half-lit warehouse of memory, tossing aside lamps, card tables and bookshelves in a futile effort to discover the sound ticking beneath stacked sofas and cigarette-scarred armchairs with their insides unrolling like yesterday's clouds.

If I wrote **now** on the next page, it would squat there like a green frog with glittering gold eyes, waiting, and the moment I touched it with my pen-point, it would jump back to the previous page.

I would have to chant **Now Now Now** endlessly, if I wanted it to occur now, and I wouldn't have time or space to write or think or do anything else.

I breathe now. I fry an egg now. I put my shoes on now. I walk into the street....Now you can see my difficulty: I am writing to you this instant; I am always writing to you this instant, writing about this place where I am and you are and how important, trivial, marvelous, terrible, futile, sad, or joyous this place is. But you never get to read my words until now, when it's already later and I'm somewhere else—in fact, where I am now.

CULTURE

Whenever I fall into despair over the behavior of my fellow humans, I am turned away from bitterness by thinking of the word *culture*, that totality of everything we've learned and done and pass on to the future in the arts, politics, religious beliefs, manners, commerce, science, and architecture, and which, whether we are aware of it or not, we express in our cities, nations, inventions, machines, paintings and books.

Not that my spirits are raised by that, but by my remembering that *culture* is also the word we've chosen to describe the growth of micro-organisms on a dish.

FIRE

1.

Last night I saw a house go up in flames. It was a wooden family house, two stories high. The fire shot from windows and walls, spiraling around the peaked roof. The firemen discussed how to control it, directed each other to do this and that, and finally stood as I did, watching in silence, helpless and awed. The flames were like the hair of a god whose face was lost inside the house, where it chewed voraciously, as if feasting on the innards of a felled beast, and yet with each bite the god seemed to be devouring itself.

2.

This image had occurred to me years before when I watched an old apartment building burn out of control in the middle of a city. Then it seemed a god had gotten loose inside and was raving against his creation. The firemen watched in the same way they did last night, silent, staring, just like the crowd behind them, and I imagined they were all thinking in their own way about how helpless we were, and how all we could do was look on amazed, almost hypnotized, as the fire showed us how little in this life we control.

3.

Their cast-off armor littering the dunes and plains around Troy, the Greeks watched the city's walls and battlements go up in flames, unwilling or unable to put them out, while a man—holding his young son's hand, and carrying his father on his shoulders, his wife lost somewhere in the mayhem behind him—stole from the city by a secret passage to wend his way from island to island, shore to shore, following the gods' directions, as they led him silently, irrevocably, to settle near the seven hills that one day would be Rome.

4.

The first thing the Goths did when they breached the walls of Rome was set it on fire. They ran helter skelter through the Salurian Gate in their furs and harness, shouting and roaring, torching the nearest buildings. The raping and plundering came later, as did the pitiless murders, despite Alaric's orders to refrain from brutalizing the populace. The fire scampered all the way to the Palatine Hill, although it didn't consume the Senate. It's true that Rome remained standing and Alaric was gone with his wagonloads of booty in six days. But it was the beginning of another end.

5.

In Alexandria, the Library went up in flames. The shelves of scrolls, like miles of perched birds, for a moment fluttered on fiery wings and then collapsed into ash: all the accumulated words of the past, all the prayers to forgotten gods, breathed their last, leaving us on rafts of personal knowledge—a few logs lashed together with hemp and gut—adrift on a cold black sea under a sky littered with unreadable stars.

6.

When asked why he had ordered the burning of the Library, the conqueror, with a shrug, said that true knowledge was written in the book of his god. All other learning was false and therefore unnecessary. The many descriptions written of the Library burning down, including mine, are apocryphal. The building and all its wisdom didn't go up in a whooshing bonfire. So "unnecessary" was the collection to the conqueror, he ordered the 700,000 scrolls burned as fuel to heat the city's public baths. It took six months to burn them all.

7.

In 881, the poet Wei Chuang watched the rebel army, "raging like stampeding beasts," enter Ch'ang-an, the Imperial City, and "choke the broad avenues with smoke from roaring fires." The many-colored tapestries and silken banners on the public buildings, the Han Yuan Palace with its staircases of gold and lapis lazuli, the mansions with vermillion gates, and West Market—with its narrow streets of peddlers, tea houses, wineshops, and its odors of lacquer, ceremonial incense, and butchers' stalls—all went up in flames, as the rebel sword blades launched "fountains of boiling blood" into the air, and severed heads rolled in the streets, their dimming eyes—questioning? imploring? disbelieving?—staring at the sunny sky.

8.

When the conquistadors torched Tenochtitlan in 1521, four million birds went up in flame. Bird cages and aviaries all over the city were baskets of fire, jails of fire—a conflagration of trapped birdsong shrieking into ashes. This city Cortés had called "the most beautiful thing in the world" and then leveled, filling the canals and causeways with the houses' adobe bricks and the palaces' blocks of red volcanic rock, was soon a mound of rubble. The great stone temples rose scorched and empty over the debris. Three years later, the Franciscan monks directed the converted populace to pull down every temple in the land, reducing the city's gods and the gods of the earth to dust and ashes, so their one god could rise to heaven on his cross.

9.

While cremating Shelley's body on the beach at Viareggio, Trelawny observed that the poet's heart would not burn. The bones had long since charred and turned to ash, but the heart sat in a pool of its own oil, a blue flame around it, as if it were a holy lamp burning for us all, and Trelawny reached into the fire and grabbed it. What was he thinking? Was he trying to grasp the poet's immortality, that eternal quality he imagined would not allow the heart to be consumed? Was he trying to find, in that spontaneous gesture, the poet's essence, the source of the prophetic voice, an imagined connection to the gods? He shrieked and sprang backward, dropping the heart, watching it sputter and pop among the coals, a lump of meat, a transforming chunk of molten energy without words or song.

10.

The two old men, both Aborigines, emanated a chalky pallor from beneath their black skins. Might they trouble me for a fire? they asked, nodding to the fireplace in the living room. It had been five days since they'd arrived in America on a cultural exchange, and in all that time, they explained, they "hadn't had a single blaze."

Ten minutes later they sat cross-legged on the tiny hearth, muttering to each other and leaning toward the flaming logs, their backs to me and the other guests at the breakfast table. When they rose in half an hour, the pallor was gone and they came to the table all smiles and quiet charm. "Fire's their spiritual oxygen," the interpreter said. "They haven't been in a house with a fireplace since they arrived, and they'd been feeling so ill they'd contemplated building a fire on their last host's lawn."

11.

Who are the gods that rule us? I say they go by the names of Chance and Whim. The first we can do nothing about, but the second lives inside us, clenching and unclenching like a restless fist.

12.

Sometimes I sense a god in me, snorting in my vitals, his jaws sunk into my bowels, wrenching his head this way and that as if he would tear something loose. I am the house he's targeted for burning, this god who is neither divine nor abstruse, whose language is inspired by the shadows on the river of my blood and whose words singe my tongue when they rush from my mouth.

13.

Blood circles the body. Smoke rises from the river. Night birds shriek in the trees. Flaming wings flare from the darkness, where drums are not distant waterfalls but the incessant footfalls of the gods.

14.

Fire clings, the Chinese say. Its radiance is accompanied by the shadow it clings to, the smoke and ash that's left of the wall or body the vines of fire climbed and embraced and collapsed with into ashes.

15.

The god who lives in each of us will not let us go. He loves and hates us. Each of us is the shadow he clings to. Our only solace is knowing that if he lives on our breath, he dies without it.

16.

The phoenix builds its nest of frankincense and myrrh, and sings about its death as it works. Then it sits in its nest and its wings fan the nest into fire. Soon you can't tell its feathers from the flames. It burns until only ashes remain, but from the ashes it rises iridescent pink and blue and gold and whole again.

17.

Feathers of fire straining to break into flight, feathers held down by the body they cling to. Flames like droplets of blood. Vines of fire climbing my bones, as with these words the breath flames from my throat.

18.

Is it the same burning in us that leads us to murder as well as to create, to torch as well as sing, and sometimes, in ecstasy, to do both at once?

19.

I keep coming back to words, as if it is important that the breath flaming from my throat say something meaningful about the dead and what they hoped for when alive, and about the repetitions of words and events and the fires that in the end burn our words and events to ashes. Our gods are not merciful. They kindle torches inside us. They speak to us through that fire, or we speak through it, as if we or they are enraged at what we are or what we have become.

20.

What do these gods want from us? What did they expect? What is it about us that so enrages them and even enrages us? The god who lives in me thumps against his prison bars, not shaking them as if demanding his release, but maintaining a steady beat as if constantly reminding me that he is there, as if his rage, like mine, is not about death but about life becoming death, the flames that at any moment may steal our breath.

21.
What are these words that will turn to ashes trying to do—remind me not to forget that life is becoming death?

22.
The body burns down and the imprisoned god burns with it. The words burn down and their meanings burn down with them. And no bird rises from those ashes.

23.
What words then do I sing as I lumber toward my bonfire of vanities—do we sing? What words can guide us?—because that's what words do. And what words can we believe in?

24.
Some days I think the fire that burns in me is stoked not in the malice of a personal god but in the furnace of my beast heart, and that heart is the reminder of the burning coal, the fiery fragment that continually ignites the eternal dark.

25.
Other days, I think the universe, like blind Samson trudging endlessly around his millstone, revolves around its secrets while unknowingly grinding worlds to dust.

26.
I am like the firemen who were unable to stop the two buildings from burning: I stand between my choices helpless and awed—but not silent.

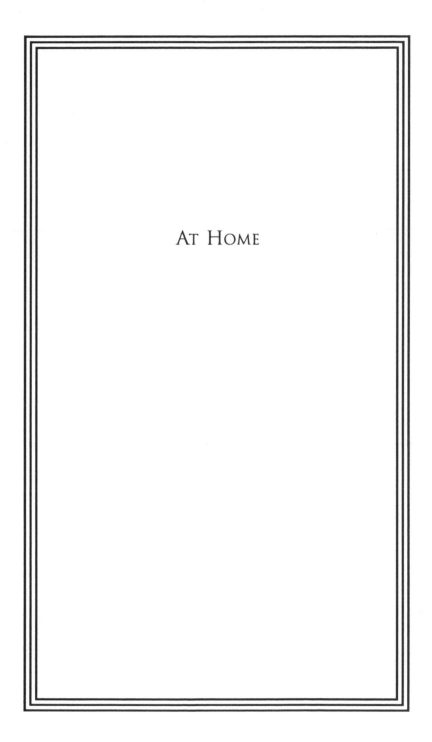

AT HOME

THE BOOTS IN MY UNCLE'S CLOSET

My grandfather is disappearing into his boots as he trudges across the Polish border. It is a smoky winter morning in 1909. Over his shoulder, he carries a burlap sack bulky with family heirlooms that he's taking to America for safekeeping—wine cups and candlesticks, a silver coffee set, his mother's golden wedding ring. But with every thunk of his heel, he sinks deeper into the boots, as if they were tunnels under the earth that give way to new depths with each imprint of his moist white feet.

With every step, the boots are rising on my grandfather's legs. Soon he will be engulfed by them, but he seems not to notice. With the sack pressing into his shoulder, he continues tramping toward the port city of Bremen in his chest-high boots.

Does he know where Bremen is? Will there be anything left of him by the time he arrives, or will he have to haul himself up to peek over his boot tops, as if over a hill, to see the ships and bales of cargo on the wharf?

This is the story of my grandfather's week-long trek to Bremen that will be repeated again and again to the generations of children in the family. In some versions, the boots will make the journey on their own. In others, Grandfather stands inside them as in the conning tower of a submarine, peering straight ahead, directing them where to go with a determination that can only be termed heroic.

In America, meanwhile, his children and grandchildren stare at the ocean, tense, expectant, waiting for the old man and his boots to appear over the horizon, so their lives can begin.

The Girl Who Became My Grandmother

Every night after the household was asleep, the girl who became my grandmother rode her stove through the forests of Lithuania.

She would return by dawn, her black hair gleaming with droplets of dew and her burlap sack filled with fog-webbed mushrooms and roots.

"It's true," my grandfather said. "At first I followed, but I could never keep up." He would hear the clanging and rusty squeakings fade into the trees and, with a sigh, he would go home.

He accepted the situation until the night she left in the kitchen, as if she rode in a coach pulled by black horses of wind.

Grandfather followed in the rest of the house, standing in the doorway to the now-departed room, bellowing threats as if urging the house forward at greater speed.

He caught her outside Vilna, when she stopped to get her bearings, and the house slammed into the stalled kitchen, grandfather tumbling through the doorway and hitting his head on the leg of a table.

"And where do you think you're going this time, Lady?" he groaned from the floor, rubbing his right ear.

The girl smiled down at him and, kneeling by his side, stroked his hair, but didn't say anything.

That was the last time the girl who became my grandmother went on a nocturnal outing. Soon after, they left for America.

In Brooklyn, she rode from one day to the next in the house he had built around her, watching the changing scene beyond the kitchen window.

It was then she became my grandmother, white-haired and smiling, never saying much of anything, even when the old man shouted from the other rooms. Not that he ever needed anything. He just wanted to be sure she was still there.

WAKING

Like a land mass rising from the sea, our faces—nose, brows, cheeks—emerge from sleep with a gasp, twin spouts of air whooshing from nostrils, echoes of sea caves bellowing from throat and mouth.

Sensations sluice down rib cages, between legs and arms, crashing against fjords and cliff walls, and we sense the outline of our bodies wherever the tingling rushes and withdraws.

Water, in the end, is our only memory. Mermaids stream through our heads, tenuous as currents, as we lie on our backs, uncertain if we can rise, wondering if we are the land or the person who dreamt the previous day into an existence we can no longer remember, aware only of our arms and legs outstretched beyond our bodies.

This is the moment we forget when we are fully awake—that terror we experience the instant before we open our eyes, not knowing if we will be staring at the ceiling or the sky.

WHAT'S IN A NAME

My family thinks I'm a pessimist. "There he goes again," my wife and daughters say, rolling their eyes, when I mention an airline crash or predict the end of the Republic.

It's been going on a long time, and I'm sure it's because of my name. "Morbid," my mother said so often when I was a boy—"you're morbid"—that I thought she was teaching me my first name, as if I were an idiot who couldn't remember how to pronounce it.

"Mort is death in French," Henry Franklin explained in the schoolyard when we were ten, and smirked when he said it. I walloped him good, but was secretly proud that unlike the Henrys, Joes, and Jacks, my name meant something in the scheme of things.

Actually, I'm neither a pessimist nor an optimist. I just envision the clean-up for the birthday party before we order the cake, and the stacks of dirty dishes before we set the table.

I'm not arguing here in my defense, but it's a little disconcerting that when a friend calls, "Hey, Mort," and I turn, his face is falling inward and he is being whisked backward into the eternal darkness before I can say hello. Now when someone calls a greeting, I shrug and mutter "goodbye" before I turn to see who it is.

I don't want to make too much of all this, though. Let's leave it at me being just like you with my aches and complaints. But as for things turning out for the best, or you having a good day—I wouldn't count on it.

THE BREAD OF MY LIFE

When I was a boy and hungry all the time in the boarding schools, I thought that the winter fields beyond the windows were covered by large slices of white bread, and that everywhere on the planet people could step from their front doors and break off a piece whenever they were hungry. I thought the Eskimos must be the jolliest of people, their moon faces always smiling, because they were surrounded by more bread than anyone else, and I reasoned that the bears and seals they lived among were white because they had eaten so much bread.

Too young to go out and play, I watched the other kids let loose in the fields, and saw how they screamed and ran and giggled as they threw the snow at each other without making it into balls, and how almost every one of them would halt now and then to feed themselves handfuls of snow like hunks of birthday cake, or how they would hold out fistfuls of snow for their friends to eat, maintaining their posture, focused, concerned, as they watched their companions feeding like ponies from their hands.

What was I—four, five years old? I already knew I was alone in the world—but so what, if the earth was bread for us all.

The next year, I was let loose with the others in the year's first snow. I ran into the fields laughing and screaming just like them, only to find that the world was a colder place than I had imagined.

I don't want to exaggerate: the other kids were often cruel and insensitive, but even now I find myself holding my breath when I remember them running through the white fields and pausing to feed each other handfuls of snow.

MY FATHER'S HOBBY

My father's hobby—don't laugh—was collecting sneezes. No stamps or coins for him. "The stuff of life," he said, "of life."

My mother and brothers shook their heads, his friends smirked, but he hurt no one, was an honest electrician, and everyone eventually shrugged it off as a harmless quirk. As his closest friend, Manny Borack, told my mom, "It could be worse."

Dad would mount the sneezes on glass slides he carried in his pockets everywhere he went. Some sneezes resembled flower petals, others seafoam, amoebas, insect wings, still others fan-shaped foetal hands, splatters of raindrops, or empty cocoons.

Next he stained the specimens magenta, turquoise, egg-yolk yellow, and placed them in the glass cases that stood in all the rooms.

Late at night when the family slept, he'd arrange handfuls of the slides on the light table in his study, and, switching off the lamp, he would peer down at them and smile.

One night, a small boy with bad dreams, I crept terrified through the darkened house to the study. He was bent over his collection, his face, surrounded by darkness, glowing in the table's light, as his lips murmured something again and again.

I slid my small hand into his and listened. He was rocking back and forth, bowing to the slides. "God bless you," he was saying, "God bless."

A Treatise on Time

Elves came each night with fresh packets of time strapped to their backs. While everyone slept, they'd shovel out the previous day's radiant dust from all the clocks in the house, and insert the packets without waking us up. Sometimes they'd stay with wrenches and oil cans, adjusting ratchets and flywheels, tapping silver hammers on metal shafts, and polishing time's mechanical heart. But they were always careful, in the end, to sweep up and carry away the filings that remained of their work, as well as yesterday's dust.

It was evident that the elves were repairmen of some kind, or maintenance workers in the employ of a company that had been contracted to care for the world's clocks.

The entire enterprise suggested a corporate structure that loomed high above with the complexity of the starry sky. When I asked my father how it worked, he patted my head. "That's big business," he said. "You're learning good."

"But what happens to all the shiny specks of yesterday's dust the elves clean up?"

My mother smiled. "They take them away so little boys won't pick them up and have time on their hands," she said. "Now up to bed with you. Go on."

So it was back to sleep with the riddling dichotomy of business and idleness wrestling in my brain, and the elves at work again downstairs after my parents had turned out the lights and the house was still. Soon the living room was filled with trapezoids of moonlight and blocks of shadow, and radiant filings were stacked everywhere on the carpet like dunes of metallic sand that pinged through my dreams.

By morning, those dunes would be gone, swept up and carted to the edges of space, where a great cliff surrounded the universe, at

72

the bottom of which lay a dumping ground of capsized wooden hulls and palace walls rising from a welter of baby carriages and listing refrigerators with gaping doors.

I had it all figured out by the time I was ten, without my parents' help. Big business had nothing to do with it, nor did my mother's concern with idle hands. Time and the universe were corporations all right, although it was never clear if time was a subsidiary of the universe, or the universe a subsidiary of time, and after a while it didn't matter which was which, or even if both of them didn't exist. All I could be sure of—all I cared about, really—was that I stood on this great island grinding through night and day, leaving the garbage lot of the past in its wake.

Older now, a lifetime of notions diminishing behind me, I suspect there must be a whole city glittering in every moment, and instead of that moment being left behind, it must sail with us through the universe like an ocean liner stippling the darkness with the faint sounds of lost voices and forgotten orchestras, sounds which rise only a short distance and double back to wrap the ship in its individual moment—one moment in an endless armada of moments that float through the universe like incidents the universe cannot forget.

THE HEAD

for Kim Wolterbeek

My Uncle Ernie found a head in his bowling ball case. It was nearly a perfect fit, a "mob job. Probably drugs," said the cop as he flipped over the pages of his pad and tucked it into his shirt pocket.

Every time he bowled after that, my uncle couldn't avoid the notion that he was poking his fingers into the victim's nostrils and mouth. It put him off his game, and more often than not the ball would roll into the gutter.

"That's where they all wind up," his friend Solly said with a grin, "in the gutter," and he went rat-a-tat-tat with an imaginary machine gun.

My uncle didn't think that was funny, that and the other jokes about the Headless Horseman or how good it was that he was finally "getting ahead in the world."

"For chrissake! For chrissake!" he'd say, and "Let a guy have some peace. They don't even know who he is, for chrissake." But I couldn't understand if the guy he referred to was the victim or himself.

"Victim? What do they mean by that? He was someone. He coulda had a wife, maybe kids," my uncle said one Sunday at the family dinner.

"Take it easy," my father said, nodding to the other end of the table, where my grandmother sat. "Mama—remember?" But the old lady was patting my sister's hair and smiling, and hadn't heard.

Uncle Ernie looked at her, then leaned close to my father. "I mean, who was the guy, and how did his head get in my case?" he said in a scratchy whisper.

My father shrugged. He was the oldest of three brothers and the others were always asking him questions, which he inevitably answered with a shrug. "Coulda been anyone," he said. "You still keep the case in your locker at work?"

Uncle Ernie nodded.

"Coulda been anyone," my father said again. "You can't think about it no more. Forget it."

But Uncle Ernie couldn't forget it. After school, I'd meet him when he got off work at the post office, and he'd drive me home. "They don't understand," he'd say, leaning toward me from the steering wheel. "Everyone else has a locker. Why mine? See what I mean? There's more to this than your dad thinks."

The kids at school knew about the head from their parents, and crowded around, asking if I'd seen it, and what Uncle Ernie had said about it. That was the year Mr. Goodman told the class about head-hunters in the Amazon, how they shrunk the heads and sewed the lips together and stitched the eyelids shut.

Shortly afterwards I began dreaming about the head. A hand was holding it by the hair in front of my face. The sewn lips were struggling against the threads, wanting to say something, and the eyelids fluttered and flew off like two moths, leaving the eyeballs bloodshot and swollen, staring into my eyes, as if the head was beseeching me to explain why it was unable to speak.

In two or three months the jokes and questions stopped, and my uncle's bowling game improved. It was about that time he met Aunt Sue, to whom, my father said with a smirk, he lost his head. After they married and had kids, Uncle Ernie would answer any questions, even questions about the head, with a shrug.

Eventually the head came to mean all the unanswered questions everyone had asked about it, even when the cop arrived at the house several months later and told Uncle Ernie and my father who the head belonged to. They shrugged. But I was too young to shrug. Besides, I had this weird idea that if I shrugged my head would fall off.

BLACKBOARDS

Like the rest of the kids, I threw spit balls and giggled, wiggling in my desk that was lined up with all the others in front of a blackboard running the length of the classroom wall. But to me that blackboard was not part of the wall; it was a window opening onto the universe, and the teacher's hand was God's writing on the darkness, and the white words or complex mathematical equations were stars and constellations as permanent as any zodiac in the heavens.

Even as an adult, I continue to view celestial maps as I did blackboards when I was a boy, and look at astronomers as teachers who connect the white dots for us with white lines, chalking human figures on our nights: hunters, virgins, mythical beasts, who perform every act in life's drama as they slide across the sky, their shapes as unchanging as the passions they depict.

Those figures are our gods—Greek, Norse, Hindu, Chinese—who parade our imperfections across the night like giant movie stars, or like those shadowy beings, masked and wigged, who wander through our sleep, projecting fun-house mirror images of our darkest secrets and fears.

Students, movie-goers, whoever we may be, we sit rapt and breathless, following every turn of the plot, and we batter our hands together when the sun's golden rays lower their curtain on the darkened stage, never tiring of the same stories night after night, stories we perform each day, forgetting that we're not imitating the starry figures, but creating the tales that each night they enact.

When these gods and their victims chase, rape, murder, and strut the heroic deeds and political trickery that made them famous, we are charting our frailties among the stars for all to see, as if we were advertising our follies to the heavens like children bragging about their naughty deeds—children just like you and me, who giggled and squirmed and threw spitballs at each other in front of the blackboard that stood silent on the classroom wall.

KISSES

When I was a boy, the kiss waited in the hall or around the corner, always outside the classroom where our voices droned.

When I was awake it hovered in my dreams, and when I slept it fluttered beside my bed, holding its breath.

I could tell you that the kiss was like a butterfly, but you've probably already thought of that.

Of course, there was more than one, there was a skyful of kisses migrating toward me from another hemisphere, but they hadn't arrived, not yet. They were just over the horizon, although their perfume billowed ahead, engulfing me in clouds of cidery scents that watered my eyes and tugged away my breath.

Each spring the kisses hid behind bushes and trees, but even though I dashed from trunk to trunk, even though I heard the beating of their wings, I could never find them.

Then all at once they appeared, swarming over me until I couldn't breathe—not butterflies, but a yapping kennel of kisses, all on show, and I was the judge. There was the woman walking her poodle kiss, snout in the air; another with her bulldog growling in my face; and a third with her nibbling Pekingese.

Then came the lion-licking kisses, the bear-nuzzling, pig-rooting, horse-teeth kisses;

kisses like sharks and barracuda sliding around a drowning man and bumping against him, or piranha kisses that shot straight at me, clicking their spiky teeth.

There were deep-throated lily kisses, open-mouthed orchid and daffodil kisses;

rainstorms of kisses, blizzards of kisses, hurricanes, typhoons, tornados of kisses.

Kisses, kisses—kisses finally cold and far away.

In the end it was wind-swept planet kisses, sun-spurt kisses, showers of static, cosmic belches and glittering galaxy kisses, kisses like star systems erupting as soundlessly as exploding hearts, icy-black silence kisses, and faint, almost imperceptible radio-signal kisses that twitter even now from deep in the night and wake our children and grandchildren with a start.

When God said, "Let there be light," his lips kissed each other, some people say, and the spark from that contact flared through the dark and was the first day.

THE DANCE

I said "No!" to my parents and left the house. I said "No!" to the boss and kept my moustache.

Then I saw her at the bus stop. I rushed toward her there, and then in the park. Each time, a wind shoved me forward, then tugged me back.

She was thrust toward me, and withdrawn before we could touch.

Her arms streamed outward, her black hair whirled: it was a frantic dance.

Finally, she clung to me, I clung to her. Around us the air collapsed, then reassembled, and we woke in a room formed by our bodies. A wind surrounded the room.

Now each night we clutch and cling in this room. Our vibrations create other rooms that surround this one, until a house surrounds us. And, needless to say, a wind surrounds the house.

Above our room, my parents, sitting in a trunk, paddle back and forth across the attic floor. "Don't worry, Mother," my father calls, "the outrigger is the safest canoe there is." They are conditioning themselves for the vacation they've saved for all their lives.

We hear them scraping across the ceiling, chanting, "No-no! No-no!" or crooning versions of South Seas love songs that were popular when they were young. Sometimes they rock the trunk from side to side while practicing what I suppose must be a variation of the hula.

Below, we buck and cling, although at times, as a novelty, we adjust our rhythms to the scraping sounds above.

Children shout in distant rooms. Beyond the windows, voices call, cars rumble and roar. Around them all, a wind drones.

"Darling, a neighborhood is growing up around us," my woman sighs.

I don't reply. But, damn it, I suspect it's more than that.

WHAT FATHERS DO

My wife tells me that when she was a little girl, her father would ask, "Where's the ocean?" And she'd squinch her face, turn her head this way and that, point in the imagined direction, and say, "There!"

Riding in the Oldsmobile station wagon, standing outside his auto parts store, or carrying bags of groceries in the supermarket parking lot, he'd suddenly say, "Where's the ocean?" and she'd squinch her eyes, giggle and point: "There!"

It was a game they played year after year, although they lived less than a mile from the ocean, and deep in the night could hear it whispering below the bark of sea lions chipping at the darkness.

"Why do you think he kept asking you that?" I say.

"So I'd never be lost," she answers.

I nod and smile.

She observes the smile. "Why do *you* think?"

"It's what fathers do," I say.

MONSTERS

My daughter asks, "Where do monsters come from, Daddy?" I raise my arms and growl. She shrieks, then giggles and punches me playfully in the chest. "No, *real* monsters," she says, and pushes me in the chest again, this time as if urging me to take her to their place of origin.

I shuffle to the den, take down a book with a photograph of Hitler in it. She contemplates the moustache, the hairdo, the flat, expressionless eyes. "He's a man *too*," she says, as if I'd tried to fool her.

She ruffles through the pages and comes upon a gloating Mussolini —shaved head, lower jaw thrust out, arms looped together across his chest. She grins as she does at television cartoons, but says, "No, Daddy: *monsters!*" and heaves the book with both hands onto the couch beside her.

I raise my arms again and growl. She giggles in response. And I am both happy and sad that she is unable to understand the lesson she has just taught me.

Discord

When I argued with my wife, I remembered her love of snow-storms. Later I couldn't forget how she had filled the kettle between us with stew—all that old meat and leftover vegetables she kept dragging up and throwing in—so at the next blizzard I wished the snow would turn into teeth, and hearing a clatter on the roof, I tapped out my pipe in time to the rhythm and went to bed with a smile.

Next day the newspapers reported that the public gardens had been destroyed: rare, irreplaceable flowers mercilessly chewed. People had been bitten on the streets; and although most of the teeth had stabbed harmlessly into hats, or into the padding in over-coat shoulders, some had ripped away cheeks, bitten through eyes, fingers, eaten at toes.

Buildings were pitted as if by shot. Properties were desolated. The rich watched values hopelessly drop. And the poor, who had no property but who could at least enjoy the snow, had what little remained of their happiness totally ruined.

Worse yet, farmlands were devastated for miles around, and famine was predicted for the following year. Even factories were damaged and a general shutdown began.

I write this in the gathering cold of a late afternoon. The lights and fuel have been out for days. Mobs in the streets are breaking windows and demanding bread, as my wife calls me down to a supper of water, crackers, and the invariable stew.

CALENDAR

I woke to cold sunlight on the window, and the squabbling of distant crowds. I followed the sound downstairs to the calendar tacked to the kitchen wall. The days of the month, small blank rectangles arranged in rows, were, I saw, windows in an apartment house, and leaning on the sills were the famous dead, presidents and poets, generals and revolutionists. Some were silently staring out at the kitchen's fragrant light, others were giving speeches, shaking their fists or yelling at the windows above and below them.

There were other, smaller sounds coming from the calendar, some almost indistinct, and I understood that each month was an apartment house waiting on its own street, with its own names at the windows, and that all twelve buildings were the principal edifices in the city of the dead.

And what of the nameless ones, I thought, those who had been neither poets nor generals, but had struggled to exist from day to day, raising families, dying from pneumonia or heartache—those who over the eons had drowned by the millions in floods or tidal waves, had been buried by earthquakes, butchered by armies, and obliterated by the visionary and the greedy; those nameless citizens who believed in a second coming, where sunlight would be as thick and sweet as honey—because one had to believe in something, or why endure it all?

Instinctively, I knew that those nameless dead were muttering behind the ones at the windows, as unassumingly sharing the apartments with their famous counterparts as they had anonymously shared their days with them when they were alive.

Now every morning when I cross off another day from the calendar, I imagine I am closing a window on the voices in that apartment for another year. But just before I place an X over the window, I pause with pen raised, and bow my head, as if listening to directions from someone I have stopped on the street.

85

ANGEL INCIDENT

An angel appeared in my study not too long ago: bedraggled, mussed hair, muttering to himself. Both wings lifted like ocean swells with every breath he drew or word he spoke. They seemed to have a life of their own; I couldn't take my eyes off them.

The angel kept muttering to himself. He was studying a crumpled, poorly folded map, the kind bought at gas stations: he opened panels and refolded them, peering repeatedly at the network of lines inside.

He knew I was there. Several times he looked up and smiled weakly—I nodded in reply—but he never asked me directions before he strolled through the wall near the window and was gone.

Of course, I never asked him if he needed help. It never occurred to me. At the time, I thought it was enough that we were in the same room together. I was wrong. We both were.

"I FIND THE LETTER"

I find the letter in a drawer, still sealed, postmarked five years ago. A letter that when opened shrieks for help, but silently—like a hand above the waves, clutching air.

I've seen him a number of times since he wrote it, but never once in word or gesture has he referred to it.

I call him three minutes later. Remarried, no longer a drunk, he says, "Your refusal to answer made me see how foolish I was and caused me to change my life."

Moments Without Names

for Robert Alexander

I think of time as a waterfall without top or bottom, a waterfall tumbling through no place, dropping up, down, spreading sideways or no ways, a frozen waterfall, a waterfall lying on its side—the Milky Way containing not stars and planets but particles, and not particles that bleat and scream, or shout hello or cheer or call for help, not particles that are small bones or twirling leaves, but rather moments without names.

A moment without a name is a pucker like a fish mouth without a fish, and the universe is an endless crowd of fish mouths sipping at the placid surface of existence that maybe reflects sunlight or starlight, or reveals in its depths pebbles and small bones, yet is neither its reflection nor its revelation but the nothingness between the two.

And every moment without a name is a falling raindrop among all the other raindrops, all those transparent sacs containing diamonds of light—valueless, transitory, gone.

Moments without names are pockets of wind, of air. Pockets without coats or shirts, hung on instants of morning or evening. Pockets with holes through which coins of sunlight and moonlight fall to become wind and air.

And moments without names are the houses we build to keep out wind and air but which, instead, merely enclose them: emptiness within and without, and windows we stare through, seeing nothing. These are the windows from which we escaped to the city when young, only to find faces like our own, faces without names, that vanished the instant we passed them on the street—faces like the one we stare at each night when the window transforms into a mirror.

We doze in the big chair at three in the afternoon, but there is no chair, no minutes, no big or small, no afternoon. That is why we wake cranky at times, with a snort or a sniff, as if we smelled the nothingness we are, that odor of mineral dampness rising from the garden beyond the window where the earth clings to the stones embedded in it. Those places where stones and earth touch are also moments without names.

Do you remember that birthday party when you were small, not only the presents and the other kids jumping up and down and screaming, not the realization that you were passing over the border from one year to another, but the moment they tied the blindfold over your eyes and placed a strip of paper with a pin through it in your hand, whirled you round and round, and set you loose to grope your way through the darkness toward what you hoped was the paper donkey tacked to the wall? Every step you took, every hesitation, every doubt was another moment, and the donkey that wasn't really a donkey, and the tail that wasn't really a tail, and the border between the years, and the years themselves were moments that were gone as quickly as they arrived.

Here's my point: none of those birthday incidents would be moments without names if you had named them, even if you only called them "blindfold," "donkey," "tail," "birthday 5," or "birthday 7." Years later, you could point to them for yourself or others, even though they snuffle, nose to the ground, shambling farther and farther from you. You see, wherever they are when you call to them, named moments will come, bounding to you from over hills and through woods, yapping and yipping, dozens of sniffers with lolling tongues, swarming into the courtyard and roaming restlessly around you, all of them awaiting your command, eager for you to name another moment. But even before you do, many of them will nudge your legs for attention with their snouts, their jaws gently offering you dead birds of unknown origin or startled animals with darting eyes, while others will wheel toward forest and ditch, raise a paw and turn statue, pointing you toward creatures you would never have noticed on your own, creatures who hide in the nearby brush or crawl through the shadows beneath the trees.

SMOKING CIGARS

When I smoke a cigar, I'm part of the earth again, but a wilder earth than municipal parks and public gardens. The wrapped brown leaves, brittle as autumn, smell like rotting fish and crumbling stone.

Even in an apartment high above the city, I become an element of the earth once more, when the cigar smoke enfolds me like the air inside a tomb.

I sit at a table opposite an empty chair when I smoke, and imagine the cigar is an earthen whistle through which I summon whatever ghost will come. Most of the time it's a leathery man, his skin as brown and thin as tobacco leaves.

We sit face to face across the table, not speaking, smoking the same cigar from opposite directions, my mouth clasping the unlit end, and his the fiery cinder whose glow must resemble the burning coal that sprang from the darkness to start the world.

He blows into the cigar as if blowing on the coal, and I suck until I am filled with the life beyond this one. When I exhale, he sips my living air through the pink nipple that scorches his tongue.

In church on Sundays, some people eat and drink the body and blood of their god. I consort with those who are less sublime, the ones who built the pyramids and tombs with their hands, and who vanished without hope of being revered or even remembered.

FLYPAPER

1.

Flypaper hung from rafters in farmhouse kitchens and vacation dining halls, amber streamers like decorations for a birthday party, studded with specks of soot that close up were the bodies of flies in every imaginable posture, as if they had hurled themselves at a swath of daylight, not realizing it was heavy as honey.

2.

When was it, returning sweaty from basketball, I stood in the doorway of the summer cabin, a teenager with the afternoon behind me, and watched the flypaper ripple above the cots like film strips hung to dry, as if each stuck fly occupied the frame of a family snapshot: a grandmother bewildered on a porch, or a grandfather stiff and glaring at a window; an aunt long dead waving the camera away, or an uncle asking with a leer for the viewer to "pick a card, any card—queen of hearts, ace of spades. Go on!"

3.

In the barracks, the flypaper swayed above the bunks, turning this way and that—much like the strippers, pelted by our whistles and wisecracks the night before, who slunk from one end of the stage to the other, their legs, one at a time—spike-heeled shoe to joggling thigh—stepping from the sequined gold gowns that hid the eternal mystery from our eyes. The wisecracks weren't what we meant. We didn't want to snicker and jeer, but, unlike those men who once raised their spears and shouted a welcome to the sun, we didn't know how to praise.

4.

In the big chair at night when I rest from reading, memories uncoil and hang, sweet and deadly, in the dark behind my eyes, attracting thoughts that want to batter against the blackness, but burrow deeper into it with each breath. There is a dance hall inside my head, half in shadow, empty, the streamers twisting from high above almost to the floor, as if a party has just ended or is about to begin, a celebration for a birth, a marriage, a death, something not of the past but from it; as if the streamers both fell to the depths and rose to the heights at the same time, twining past and future like the intricate mathematics of the double helix I find impossible to understand. They swirl this way and that like the smoke from my uncle's cigarette as he shoved the deck in my face and said, "Pick a card, any card. Go on...."

5.

In bed at night, near sleep, I imagine that my body is packed with cells, and that each cell is a city-state, and that in the center of each city-state tall apartment buildings rise full of relatives staring from the windows, and that the expressions on their faces show that my relatives believe in nothing, expect nothing, want nothing. They are just there, waiting, ready for whatever will come, as if they knew they lived in a house made of cards.

6.

These images of flypaper fall through my mind like the pomaded hairs that have fallen from my head unnoticed for years, just as memories and specks of sound must fall from the planet, strands that with space dust and sparklings drift through the universe. They are packed with information of who we were and are and will become, a message encoded in every imaginable posture, as if part of our identity is to hurl ourselves at a swath of daylight heavy as honey, muttering about the queen of hearts and the ace of spades, and our only choice is whether we intone those words with scorn or with praise.

THE REQUEST

Suddenly Bjorling's voice on the stereo: "As a request, I should like to sing for you Schubert's *Serenade*." The crowd applauds and with a cascade of piano music framing the lyrics, he sings.

But my tears had started—hot, unexpected—at hearing his words, for I was aware that the man making this announcement on the stage of Carnegie Hall in 1958, his voice clipped and formal with a foreign intonation, would be dead within two years.

Who made the request and what motivated it? A shared melody with a loved one in a long ago Vienna or Shanghai? The memory of an age moldering behind closed doors, where the faces of baroque cherubs and the tiles of upswept Chinese roofs were cracked and broken long before they were the wreckage of cities under siege?— long before millions of arms and legs twitched in mass graves? Or maybe not that. Maybe the singer—thick-chested, square-faced—having witnessed wars and depredations, was requesting permission to sing one more song for everything that was gone.

Whatever the reason, after the applause and encased in the piano's melody, the voice streaked through the hall, entered the recording apparatus, and now cleaves the heated air in my living room years later, rolling back the present on two sides to make way for its arrival from the past, like a deluge of sunlight tumbling through an opening in the clouds to the valley below, letting us glimpse for a moment a possibility of redemption in a tumult of wings.

But what's this!—the voice unexpectedly summons up the image of my father in the photograph I'd long forgotten: he poses from the waist up in a business suit, his right arm extended, as if delivering an aria, and I realize that he looked enough like this tenor I've idolized for years to be his brother—the same stocky build and beefy features—and the words I'm hearing now are coming not from the tenor's lips but from my father's half-remembered face, that face I'd seen only twice, and then for barely several minutes, and whose only words I can remember, "So, you're my son," expressed neither approval nor disapproval, just an affirmation that I existed—a statement made not for me but for himself.

But now, Father, your voice is so clear. Sing to me the old songs of love and loss and continuing on. Let your voice soothe me, an old man myself now, older than you ever were, but more in need of a lullaby on this battered earth than I ever was as a child. Sing from the past about what seems irrevocably gone but always returns, so once again I can believe in the guiding presence of fathers and the healing power of song.

Jussi Bjorling was a great tenor with the Metropolitan Opera in the 1940s & '50s.

The Story That Had Never Been Written

I first came across "The Story That Had Never Been Written" on one of those nights when the household was asleep, and I was sitting up late reading. At such times a lonely protectiveness for those dreaming in the rooms around me evokes a melancholy close to anguish, which I'm sure has something to do with the enlarged sense of time passing created by the surrounding stillness.

I had been thumbing through a short story anthology I had just bought and came across a title in the table of contents which interested me. However, when I turned to the page on which the story was supposed to begin, it wasn't there. I flipped the pages back and forth but still couldn't find it, and mildly annoyed I shut the book and went to bed.

The title in question was "The Story That Had Never Been Written," and during the next several months I found it listed in half a dozen other anthologies, but in each instance I couldn't locate the story on the page it was supposed to appear, or anywhere else in the book.

I could understand such an error happening in one volume, but the coincidence of it occurring in several was unthinkable: the omission had to be intentional.

A story without characters, without beginning, middle and end? A story that didn't exist? What did it mean? What could have drawn the editors to it? Indeed, *how* could the editors have been drawn to it?

My annoyance turned to curiosity, and finally I was intrigued.

I went to the town library and looked up the writer in a biographical dictionary, finding him mentioned in a short paragraph along with a bibliography of his books, which included three novels and a collection of stories.

His name was Elaard van Steen. He was born and had lived in a small Dutch town in the second half of the nineteenth century, where he worked as a night switchman at a railroad crossing outside of town. He had written his stories to while away the long nocturnal intervals between train passings, had never married, and had died of leukemia six months short of his fortieth year. One of his novels, *Anguish*, had achieved some attention and had been translated into French and German, but critics of his own day thought that he had not come into his full powers by the time of his death. Recently, the article concluded, his short stories had received renewed interest and he was thought by some to be a precursor of the literature that explores the "psychological condition of modern man."

I checked out the book of short stories, but refused to open it before I got home, and then only when my wife and two sons had gone to bed.

I read the book through without looking at the table of contents. The tales were generally unexceptional, except for several stylistic felicities and ironic reversals. The stories concerned what one would have expected from a switchman sitting alone with nothing to do for hours on end, as he put it, "under the constant flowering of the botanical night."

There was a story about an Arab sitting by a fire under desert stars; a Dutch rubber plantation owner in the East Indies whose wife leaves him; a young girl suffering from insomnia because when she does sleep she dreams of falling while ice skating, floundering about, and everyone around her refusing to help her up. Stories of frustrated wives, lonely children, stifled men.

I sighed and turned to the table of contents, and there to my surprise—although I can't say why—was the title of the story which had drawn me to the book in the first place. "The Story That Had Never Been Written" was listed as the twelfth of the fifteen stories, but I couldn't remember what it was about. I flipped to the indicated page and once again found nothing—or more accurately, I found what I had in the other collections, the next story listed.

The story I was looking for simply did not exist. It never had. I slammed the book shut and sat there with the sound receding in all directions through the quiet house.

My wife called dreamily to me from several rooms away, but I didn't answer. What could van Steen have been thinking of?

I pushed myself out of the chair, almost claustrophobic with annoyance, and sauntered through the house, out the back door, and into the shadowy yard.

The sky bloomed around me. I felt infinitesimally small beneath it, and I thought of van Steen seated night after night under this same sky, contemplating his aloneness and his early death.

And all at once I knew the meaning of "The Story That Had Never Been Written." It was a sign for the blankness, the emptiness of all those stories van Steen knew he would never write, maybe of all those stories that had never been written, or would never be told, by anyone else.

But van Steen had been mistaken. Viewing himself under a nineteenth-century sky, he imagined that he only had one of two choices. It never occurred to him that each choice contained not only its opposite but every other choice as well. And as I reflected on this I thought I could hear the people turning over in their beds in the houses around me. I thought I could hear them murmuring and calling out, and I was calling back that everything was all right, Don't worry, I'm here, as time grew large around me and passed me by in the stillness of the story that is always being written.

ON STREETS & ROADS

Spring Laughter

Spring laughter. An open window and someone passing, boy or girl, alone or with another, friend or lover, beyond the window.

Road or street, running or strolling, laughter rising from easy conversation or urgent whisperings. Now or in the eighteenth or nineteenth century. Here or in a Polish city or a Turkish suburb.

Laughter we have heard before and will hear again, a trill, light as birdsong, and we, seated at the kitchen table, a cup before us, recognizing, raising our heads, suddenly attentive, as the laughter—spiraling above wooden wheels clattering on cobblestones, or engines revving at the curb—disappears.

Friday, the 13th

Every day should be Friday, the 13th. Not on calendars, but in our heads.

Touching the inside knob of the front door, we should shiver, remembering there may be nothing on the other side, neither lawns nor neighborhood, merely the house perched on the edge of a cliff, the door opening onto an expanse of sun-drenched silence.

The car may have been repossessed in the night, or may now waddle off on its four tires like a toothless lion with arthritic paws.

Your penis may have flown away like a worm in the dark, or your vagina simply disappeared, and where either one was only a hump as bald as an elbow remains.

Yes, every day should be Friday, the 13th. The closed house of our habits should open its doors and windows and let us romp in the world outside.

So passing an alley after dark, look into it. There, beyond garbage cans and turned-away cats kicking spasms from their legs, a shadow may rise and open its robes that are lined with threads of golden rain, threads like pollen drifting down or the shedding of moth wings. Don't be afraid. Move closer. See how the threads are actually chains composed of minute gold spheres that spin in the darkness and whirl around each other? See how they expand the nearer you come, larger and larger, until you are floating between huge rims of humming light, and you know that once more your life is about to begin?

Departure

There is only one departure. He leaves his home town in the middle of the night, at dawn, or at noon, and is never heard from again. Or she leaves. He or she: it makes no difference. They're gone—married not to each other but to oblivion.

In the days to come, the townspeople meet in groups of two or three in drugstores and gift shops. They remember words, signs, restless gestures, incidents from the departed one's family history and character, but they are unable to determine why he or she has gone.

Did he leave with head bowed, trudging under his backpack? Did she go with sprightly step, swinging her valise by the handle? None can answer, all remember different versions, and in this way the departed one remains among them, more a presence than when he or she was there.

Now hundreds of replicas of the one who left—some smirking, some shouting at closed doors or weeping as they slide out of sight—inhabit models of the town the townspeople carry in their heads, a maze of neighborhoods, alleys and streets, from which no one can depart.

IN PASSING

We own so little in this world, not even the face in the mirror of the shop window where we glimpse ourselves passing—that look of surprise more than recognition that departs as quickly as we do, leaving the mirror empty once again.

ANGELS

for Jana

Every moment, a procession of angels glides toward us. If we look back, suddenly, from a lit street into an alley in shadow, or at breeze-tossed trees, we may see them in their robes, hands clasped together, hurrying to catch up, always sweeping in our direction, whether scooted forward by the wind or buffeted by rain or snow. When we reach back to pull them to us, however, we are unable to touch their garments or hands. But still we must try, and no matter how unbridgeable the separation, we must peer into those faces like wind-slurred water, and attempt to identify who they are, hoping in our drunkenness and blood-splattered clothes that some aspect of their features resembles our own.

THE SEDUCTION OF THE TREES

Each night the trees imitate the birds they see flying during the day. They choose the darkness so they won't be seen flapping and flouncing like elephants with the souls of ballerinas.

It's so damn sad when you want to be something other than what you are, especially trees who get to stand outdoors in all sorts of weather and never catch even a sniffle.

And isn't it a ballerina's most secret wish to stand on one leg day after day without tiring, while birds flutter and nest in showers of song on her shoulders?

All this is the wind's doing. Every hour it returns to woo the trees, who refuse again and again, but, like you and me, want to believe and are easily influenced.

GORILLA

I am assigned to play the gorilla in the annual parents' charity circus.

I don the heavy costume, a sort of deep-sea diver's suit covered with shiny black hair, and half-stooping I waddle and scoot into the arena when I'm announced.

The audience gasps. I have to be careful not to frighten the children, and with black-gloved knuckles propelling me forward across the sawdust-covered floor, I hobble to the balustrade in front of the first row, cooing and laying my head on top.

The children and their parents stare. There's no reaction, no expression. I slide along the barrier. It's the same everywhere—blank faces, as if I wasn't there.

I step back, leap into a somersault. No applause. No cheers. Silence. Everyone is staring at me, hundreds of eyes. I'm sweating inside the suit. What am I doing wrong?

I grunt, beat my chest, growl in a simulated rage, grab handfuls of sawdust, throw them in the air, then at the audience. Still no response.

I run in circles, hammer the arena floor until my hands ache inside the gloves, hear my bellowing roar challenge the silence, fill it, until I cough and gasp for air.

When I put a gloved hand to my mouth, I realize what's wrong: I forgot to put on the flat-muzzled gorilla head, and what the audience has been looking at is a balding, middle-aged man with wire-rimmed glasses, who wears an overcoat, coos and shouts and stomps in circles, soliciting laughter, applause, commiseration and fear. In short, I've been doing the one thing the audience doesn't want to see: I've been behaving just like them.

Time & Again

Time and again it begins something like this. You're in a phone booth in a central railroad terminal at rush hour, shut in and watching all the people through the window-muffled silence. They scurry to catch their trains, while you dial the number and speak to the child or lover on the other end who seems unusually distant, prompting you to ask, "Is there anyone there with you?" and they take too long to answer, "N-no." Even before that brief exchange, you wanted to throw open the phone booth door—as you do now— to the noise and clashing sounds, and step into the random paths of the people in the crowd, each person moving toward a preconceived destination, except you who sense the presence of the phone booth behind you like an upended coffin, as you try to decide which one of the many paths you'll step into, maybe are already committed to joining, maybe are already part of without knowing it. But still, just as before you placed the call, you experience the expanding emptiness in your chest, the constriction in your throat: you can't move, can't breathe, watching the paths in front of you continually collide and change direction. Then the telephone rings. Is it for you? It may be a wrong number, probably is—someone wanting a dry cleaner or a Chinese takeout. Will you answer it? Of course you will, and lifting the receiver to your ear, you hear a small voice that says without inquiry or greeting, "Don't hang up. Just listen. I was wrong. I need you so bad. I don't know what I'll do if..." But before you can speak, the line goes dead.

THE LETTER

I found the letter in a book I bought at an outdoor theatre turned flea market every weekend. It was June 1995 in a small town on the California coast.

The book was Tolstoy, *Anna Karenina*, and the letter was tucked between pages 434 and 435, where a delirious Levin, the day after he's proposed to Kitty, visits her parents' home. The letter—pinkish, sealed, not mailed, faintly redolent of talcum, like a pressed flower—was from a Sarah Harris, dated inside October, 1939.

Yes, I opened it and read how fine the trip was from Des Moines back to Cincinnati, suspecting nuances and unworded passages I had no way of understanding that went along with what I took to be the mute appeal to Carl Bigelow, 913 McKinley Avenue, Des Moines, Iowa, in the final paragraph: "There didn't seem time for me to say all the things I needed to. Do you feel the same?"

The Tolstoy was a book club's bonus edition bound in grey leatherette. Had Sarah Harris purposely placed the letter between those pages depicting Levin and Kitty's jubilant betrothal? I had no way of knowing, and refused to suppose. However, I resealed the letter, affixed fresh stamps to the envelope, and sent it on.

Hand Gestures

Thumb: *Thumbs Up*

The thumb held up above the fist like a candle flame, but not wavering or tenuous, rather squat and solid, means everything is good, in balance, working well.

The gesture is so forceful, so sure, if aimed at us we want to smile and nod in response and to forget for a moment that all that show of muscular certitude is as tenuous as the flame the thumb doesn't really resemble but which can burn it down.

> **Addendum:** Thumbs up also means, "Let him live," and was the sign the Emperor gave in the Circus Maximus so a victorious gladiator would spare his vanquished (but brave) opponent's life. The gesture demonstrated the Emperor's power over life and death, and allowed the spectators in the stands to forget that on the farthest borders in every direction from that thumb, the Empire was falling apart.

Index: *Come Here*

While the last three fingers bow their heads over the upturned palm, the index finger flexes back and forth from the second joint to the tip of the nail. This is the sign for "Come here, I want to see you."

The speed of the flexing defines the urgency of the summons. If rapid, the meaning is "Get over here, right now!" If languid, it is an invitation to delights we immediately imagine.

The meaning of either gesture is enhanced even more by the face of the one who performs it. A clenched-jawed, dull-eyed expression, accompanied by rapid flexings, commands the one it's aimed at to respond at once.

A slow, hanging smile assures rewards when the person signaled complies with the finger's request, although certain slow or enticing smiles promise embraces but then ensnare.

The slow, sensual invitation relaxes our vigilance, and is usually made by someone we think finds us attractive. The rapid flexing is often practiced by fathers or policemen.

> **Addendum:** A pointing index finger, aimed straight as a spear from above the curled pedestal of the other fingers held shut by the thumb, means, "I see you. You can't hide your thoughts from me any more than you can hide what you've done." If the thumb is raised, however, the index finger has become the barrel of a gun.

Middle: *Giving The Finger*

The pinky, ring and index fingers, their heads buried in the palm, grovel beneath the middle finger's jutting tower, while the thumb, a cruel overseer, holds the index finger down.

This means "Go to hell!" and worse: "Attach yourself to your anus and spill your seed inside!"

This is a gesture of power, not strength, which makes the person it's directed toward cower, or fills him with a fury he can hardly control, reminding him of scenes most of us have brought from Babylon and Egypt, Rome and ancient China, where the whip snapped on our backs and we labored for someone else's glory.

> **A word of caution:** Before you use this gesture, be aware that it may inspire a reaction in the person it's aimed at whose genealogical memory is a swinging fist.

Ring: O

The ring finger has no gesture. As if weighed down by the neck iron of the wedding band, it is rigid and can hardly raise his head.

But it tries, as if it wants to tell us something we do not want to hear, but since it cannot speak and has no gesture, there is no way we can comprehend what it wants us to know.

Pinky: *Raise And Curl*

The pinky lifts its head like a groundhog looking for its shadow, so it can foretell the coming of spring.

But don't be fooled: that little finger is of this world only and quickly curves into a show of elegance, a display of such vanity and self-absorption that its gesture is a signal which calls to no one but merely seeks attention for itself.

It gestures no farther than the end of the hand, as if what the hand could hold were the measure of the universe.

The Hand: *Encore*

And so the fingers grumble and plot, beckoning to one another and alternately gesturing thumbs down or thumbs up, giving each other the finger, or shooting each other dead, while the ring finger struggles to speak and raise its head and the pinky dances on the edge, performing curtsies and pirouettes, absorbed in its display of fine manners and etiquette.

How I Came to Own the World

We enter the world with nothing and leave it the same way. In between, we pile up appliances, canned foods, automobiles, bank accounts, real estate—hills of goods we stand in front of, as if posing for a photograph that shows our worth.

I owned nothing because I wanted nothing, one of the destitute in spirit as well as material wealth, until a curious thing happened: I read in the newspaper about a man who had murdered several people. The paper referred to the dead as "the murderer's victims," as if in some way he owned them.

This phrase excited me, but I had no desire to kill, rob, or maim. Still, the excitement was there, and soon I was intrigued by the idea that I could plan a murder or robbery, go through all the motions, but not commit the act.

I managed to get the floor plans of several mansions and banks, in my spare time followed unsuspecting women for months on end. I owned them. I owned everyone to whom I turned my attention, since I permitted them to keep what they had, including their lives. I stood in front of store windows, admiring the furs, paintings, television sets, thinking, "They're mine, all mine. All I have to do...."

Everyone was indebted to me, as if to a banker, for allowing them to keep their necklaces, stereos, cars. These things are theirs on loan. I finance them, so to speak.

Now I walk the streets of my city, proud of my apartment buildings, parks, and museums. I nod to all the passersby with a benevolence I never imagined I possessed. Each tilt of my head or tip of my hat signals, "Think nothing of it.... You're welcome.... Happy to do it."

I've never felt so good about myself. Of course, there are problems, decisions to be made, certain moral conundrums involving how I should allow lands and people to be treated and who should be permitted to do what to whom. But I don't want to bore you. I just wanted to let you know how I came to own the world. Run along. We'll speak again after you've had a chance to look around....

THE MYTH OF HISTORY

My friends told me that poets should turn history into myth. The models they cited were Homer, Virgil and Milton, two of them blind, one a proper Roman. They found connections, my friends said, that make our sufferings and failing flesh worth the effort, and we emerge more robust for the moment, not cured of our sufferings and the tumult of our days, but grander than in our daily lives, where we shuffle through the years in rumpled clothes.

But I wasn't interested in myth. I wanted to call the broom in the corner what it was, and the old woman in the park, surrounded by shopping bags full of empty egg cartons, by name. I wanted to record as accurately as I could the terror of the boy the instant he scraped his knee on a pavement square, and the despair of the small dark man in Sacramento who came up to me, clutching the want ads, and said, "I guess my job is being out of work."

All I write about, however, are brooms that dance like awkward girls, and empty egg cartons that when opened are full of birds that chirp and fly into the sky.

I'll be frank: I distrusted mythic stories from the start, as if at an early age I realized that Homer and Milton couldn't see the world they lived in, and that Virgil told the unlikely tale of a man who carried his father from a burning town, lost his wife among the flames, but led his son to a new and unexpected life where the man became a contented king, although his wife and father had died along the way.

Soon, however, I determined that history was lacking too. There had to be more to it than the boy, the instant his knee hit the pavement square, being as terrified as the son who held his father's hand amid the screams and flames of that ancient town; more than the unemployed man in Sacramento being equally forlorn as the father who led his family from their burning home and wandered aimlessly for years.

Wives and fathers die, and bills still have to be paid, and there's little hope of being rewarded with a decent job, let alone a crown. What remain are those flocks of birds that burst into the sky from non-existent eggs, and brooms that lurch around the room like adolescent girls behind their window shades.

I don't know much and understand less, but I'm aware that such images as these have flitted through our minds from one age to the next, without our knowing where they come from or what they mean. Instinctively, however, I sense that those tottering brooms do not so much recall a restless goddess locked inside a tree, as they do the wild sap leaping through trunk and branch on windy nights to shake itself free from its imprisonment in wood—just as widows and old men, hobbling around their solitary rooms, would wrench themselves out of their skins, if they could.

WHAT NARCISSUS SAW

Kneeling to drink in a forest clearing, Narcissus saw his face reflected in the gliding stream. Behind it, tadpoles wriggled and the feathery backs of fish swept their tails like iridescent fans in an inner current, nudging pebbles and twigs and skulls the size of nutshells downstream. One object responded to another as if caught in a spell that whirled them in a slow-motion dance toward the river, which a thousand miles away exploded into a sunlit sea. This was the vision Narcissus reached out to embrace when he fell into the water and drowned.

THE NEW NARCISSUS

I stare at the shifting images on the television screen, trying to see beyond my face. Behind my glassy reflection, shining cars and beer cans, toothpaste tubes and laundry boxes spin from a radiant emptiness and appear in driveways or on kitchen shelves, while old men hammer podiums with their fists, and one bombed-out city looks like all the others. One by one these images emerge and then are sucked into a vortex where they hurtle through tunnels toward the ocean. There they are dumped on a sandbar littered with half-buried bottles, rusty engines and plastic cups. I sense this process more than know it, mesmerized in front of the television set by the transformations that continue to unfold, until I can no longer tell the difference between the images on the screen and the reflection of my face.

VISIONS

for Deng Ming-Dao

They can happen anywhere, any time: while you're stirring a pot on the stove, reaching for a can of motor oil, or setting a bucket of empty beer bottles on the back porch. Suddenly, hundreds of stones, like tiny bells, chime all at once throughout a meadow, sunlight showers a golden rain through leaves and branches in a park, or, as the astronaut saw, looking through the window of his space ship, a bouquet of diamonds scatters like the beginning of the universe from the torn bag of piss he had just released into the empty darkness.

I said "piss" instead of "urine" not only to emphasize the half-rhyme of "released" and "darkness" but because I wanted the word to be as unexpected as the vision must have been to the startled astronaut. Besides, "urine" is too placid. It can never carve a new passageway into our consciousness. It pools in the mind, a stagnant liquid swaying in a sump that needs to be sloughed off with chunks of mud that drop from arms and legs as we stagger from the bog of our habitual perceptions.

But that's where we're always left, in the end: the place we come from and go back to—the mass of rubies in the cut glass bowl once more a basket of cherries on the kitchen table.

Even then, the visions keep unfolding, whether we are there to witness them or not. When we turn off the light and leave the kitchen, the cherries may start to glow, displaying pictures of events both past and future rippling up from their depths, like those intricately carved walnuts from the Middle Ages that when opened reveal a complete nativity scene on one side and the Crucifixion on the other. You know: Mary and the infant in the foreground, and ranged behind them wisemen, oxen, sheep, and packed beyond that, crowds of peasants—shepherds, inn keepers, wives and kids staring into the barn from beyond the windows, all of them backed by a clear, earth-scented night.

I once saw a walnut like that on display in a museum. One side was open and its interior enlarged by a strategically placed magnifying glass. It looked like a succession of Buddhist caves set in staggered mountainsides receding into the distance. Paths encircled the mountains that were connected by fragile bridges, and in the caves sat meditating monks, fifteen at first glance but increasing in number the longer I looked, each crack and striation so altering my perception that chants seemed to sprinkle the air around me as I bent closer to the case.

Nearer to home, those empty beer bottles—tumbled top to bottom in the blue plastic bucket on the back porch, and shadowed by the street light in the alley—could be eight snoring monks who have once more lost my address but almost found me.

SAINTS

The saints wanted none of this world. They tried to rid themselves of the body's yearnings any way they could, refusing to be cradled and smothered in the sights and scents around them.

Orchids, jasmine, stars of anise, birds trilling and whistling in the trees were anathema to them, and the long way the wind takes through laurel and oak on blond hillsides overlooking green seas, where sheep bells tinkle through the afternoons.

They sought deserts, deep forests where the sun never entered, rock faces of lava or limestone where they burrowed into the caves they'd made of their hearts against the things of this earth.

And they lashed themselves with metal-tipped whips, skewered their tongues with hot needles, scooped out their own eyes, attempted to scald the touch from their fingertips.

Finally, they drove princes and potentates to weigh them down with chains and burn them to ashes—and all this out of an immense love for Him and everything He had created.

THE ANSWER

I had known him years before, and here he was, in a small apartment on a shadowy side street in San Francisco, dying.

Then he had been a priest, big and jovial, a Jesuit chaplain in the Air Force, fond of risqué jokes and golf and philosophical conversation—conundrums mostly, scholastic cats' cradles of logic. "The Moslems may have had it right you know," he was fond of saying, shocking the others around the table. "We may be fated. Every move we make." And he'd sip at his glass to allow his statement time to achieve its effect.

"Father, how can you..."

"No," he'd say, and wave the objection away. "Even when we think we've acted freely—choosing God's way—our choice may have been determined from the start."

"That's Calvinism, Father."

He'd smirk and look away.

Even before I was discharged, he'd left the priesthood, and now, thirty years later, he'd looked me up and called.

"You came," he said from the single bed, his head large on the pillow. He was thin and waxen. "A poet now, as you said you'd be. Yes, I've read some things of yours and thought about our talks: free will, fate. Remember?"

I nodded.

"There comes a time when one has to live one's talk. I had to prove my choice was free. I chose to be a priest, to be God's soldier. But how did I know I chose? —No, don't interrupt: I don't have much strength." And he stopped to catch his breath. "For a long time I lived alone, a solitary, making as few choices as possible, examining even my most trivial decision to determine if I had made it. Silly, really. Not the answer by half."

He took another breath, readying himself to go on. "A period of impulsive actions followed. Whims. That was not only silly; it was irresponsible. After that, I gave up. There seemed to be no answer. And now I go to God."

I nodded, following the implications of his thought, remembering how obsessive it had been—and how alluring.

"I know what you're thinking," he said and smiled, then paused to gather what strength he had left, then smiled again, a gentle smile, and continued. "Did I choose to be ordained any more than I chose to pick up the newspaper and find your name, or had that discovery and my getting in touch with you been part of a universal plan of which you and I are infinitesimally small units and which, with countless others, we blindly follow from event to event? The argument is endless, back and forth: one side, then the other."

He licked his lips. Then the smile rose once more and struck me as almost beatific. "You've got to stop the argument in the middle, you see: go no further than one side or the other—that's the answer." He nodded, as if in agreement with his own words. "Any way you look at it, you've got to choose. I *chose* the priesthood. I *chose* to pick up the newspaper."

He stopped for breath again. Then wistfully, almost with a sigh, he said, "It's taken me a lifetime to learn that."

THE TRICK

When the park closes each day, managers, docents, and gardeners—as well as those who clean the cages—remove sections of the chain-link fences and don them like knights' mail. Then they pull bars, big as lances, from zoo cages, and hunt each other among the trees and shrubbery broadening with shadows. *Chink-chink* echoes through the darkness from one end of the park to the other, and these sounds are accompanied by the ponderous tolling of metal against metal. "Gotcha!" is heard now and again, and occasional giggles. Secretaries, perfumed handkerchiefs trailing from their fingers, peer anxiously from high places. Animals trot through the surrounding darkness, snuffling and snorting. When the park opens the next day, however, the animals are in their cages, bars and fences back in place, and the workers are going about their chores. The trick is to know the points of detachment and reattachment for the bars and chain-link fences. That is always the trick. The only one.

WAITRESSES

Late at night, lonely men—truck drivers, unshaven hitchhikers to anywhere, or college boys half-drunk on being eighteen—watch them approach with their bouffant hairdos and swinging hips, and imagine pumping into them on beds like slowly revolving carousels.

These are the women who wait with pad and pencil to take down anything the men want. The young ones leave their top buttons undone, know the whole room loves them, and write the orders like *billets-doux*. The older ones, when business is slow, sit at the counter, tap their cigarettes in plastic ashtrays, and stare at the darkness beyond the windowpanes.

The banter that goes back and forth between these women and the seated men is a half-remembered ritual that mimics the prescribed dialogues that took place in Hindu and Egyptian temples thousands of years ago, when diaphanously gowned priestesses of Annapurna or Isis, rubies and emeralds glittering in their hair, received the pleas of dusty, wild-eyed supplicants, and later when delicate damsels, in a dream of castles, listened to the scorching passions of delirious young men.

In Oregon or Kansas, wind and rain buffeting the plate glass windows, the men ask for fried eggs and coffee, orange juice, bacon and potatoes, meaning something else, something they've forgotten how to put into words but hope the waitresses are writing down, trusting that these women understand what they really want to say.

When the waitresses saunter from the table with their requests, the men follow them with their eyes to the chamber of fires, where cymbals clang and holy oils smoke, where birds' eggs are broken and cooked, meats from sacrificial animals prepared, and the elixirs and steaming potions brewed that will send these pilgrims into the night once more, ready to travel separate roads in search of holy places, the image of these women at roadside stops shining in their heads like the holy medallions swinging from their rearview mirrors.

THE ULTIMATE PLACE OF EXILE

Whenever I find myself about to knock people's hats off in the street or to shake my fist against the night, I think of going into exile.

Siberia, with its white winds swirling over the brittle tundra, or the Antarctic, with its glinting hills of chilly silence, are too civilized.

What I'm looking for is the most remote, the ultimate place of exile. I deserve nothing less.

At about this point I remember my elbows, those barren peninsulas jutting out into the universe, the most ignored parts of our bodies.

They are as far from our thoughts as Australia and Timbuktu, and Easter Island and Tierra del Fuego aren't nearly as remote. Nor does it make a difference if we choose one elbow or the other, since both are equally desolate.

Neither tropical nor arctic, jungle nor desert, the elbows are continents of calcified waste rarely visited by sun or moon and almost always covered with fog as dense as wool or thin as cotton.

They are the places of continual solitude, where nothing happens until they whack a doorknob or a table-end, and, more shocked than surprised, we howl like a sleeping dog awakened by sirens. In fact, it's only on those occasions that we remember our elbows exist at all.

Yes, I conclude, the elbows are the ultimate place of exile.

Then a strange thing happens. Like a shipwrecked sailor who explores the rocky island where he wakes, once I become aware of my elbows they occupy all my thoughts.

As if for the first time, I realize they are promontories of bone hinging our upper and lower arms, so our hands can reach and our arms embrace.

They are also like two skulls, as if God had run out of parts in making us and, having to improvise, had capped those hinges with the cranial coverings of infants who died the day they were born.

At the same time, He had the sensitivity to place the elbows where we cannot see them, and kept them from our thoughts until those moments when we need to remember they are there.

And what is there to remember except those unlived lives that are attached to our own so we could touch and embrace others who are equally alive and reaching out to us?

I mean, is there any act more affectionate, more gentle, than reaching for and holding the one you love by the elbows? Notice the gasp at first, or the shudder, at the unexpectedness of it, and then the softening of the other person's body, as if you had touched the secret place where hardness ends and vulnerability begins.

When I reach this thought, I am ready to come back into the world. I am ready to return from my exile.

THE DISTANT PEOPLE

The dead are not so far away. They stand in the shade under the trees across the field and watch us laugh and chase each other in the sunlight.

When I was a boy, I called them the distant people. They were always there, a presence I could hardly see but knew were watching.

They weren't like parents, waiting to scold or warn or protect — but like an assembly keeping vigil.

They spoke to me. I was sure of that. The wind carried scraps of their words, but nothing I could understand. Encouragements, I supposed, or advice. Or maybe they were talking among themselves, the way old people do when looking after grandchildren in playgrounds or overseeing them from farmhouse porches, talk full of parasols and horse-drawn carriages, great droughts and poor yields, prices falling and profits that have disappeared.

What was important was that they were there, watching over me from a distance. Whatever words they said were secondary to the reassurance their presence provided during my early years.

One day I set off across the field to meet them. It was momentous, a journey in short pants, but a journey nonetheless, a trek with determined strides, a canteen of water strapped to my shoulder and four graham crackers in a brown bag.

Their voices rose in volume the closer I trudged—a warning or a welcome, I couldn't tell which, but my heart soared. Their shadowy shapes under the trees separated and turned and motioned me forward, in time to the branches rising and dipping overhead.

When I arrived at the treeline, there was nobody there, just shadows and sunlight, sunlight and wind. I stood among the shifting shapes of afternoon and knew I should never have come, an orphan under the trees, accompanied by shadows, wind, and sun-lit air. I stayed for a while, certainly dejected, but as bewildered as I was sad, and then I went home.

When I looked the next day, I was overjoyed to see they were there again, across the field, whispering and mingling under the trees, and once more I set out to meet them—with the same result as before.

Eventually I learned to keep my distance and be content to observe them from afar. It was enough to look up from study or play and know they were there. Even now while hiking through meadows or sitting in passing cars, I see them under the trees and experience a serenity I can't explain.

Not that I need their presence or solicitude any longer, but in recent years I've come to believe that now it is my turn to look after them.

I realized a long time ago that I wasn't really an orphan. Birds in the sky, beasts in the fields, the fields themselves, and all the two-legged creatures just like me—they dance around us, sharing the places we enter and leave. They decorate our existence, as we do theirs. Everything's reciprocal. Everything is coming and going, departing and arriving, and that's why now it's my turn to watch over them.

Understand, I am not so much a guardian of all the others in this time and place as a caretaker for those that have come and gone, an advocate for sunlight and shadows, shadows and wind.

Men Who Cry

for George Ow, Jr.

1.

My stepfather was the first I knew who did. A square-faced man with a broken nose who beat my mother and was always ready with a curse or a fist, he blubbered when the woman in the black dress, big as the side of a building, sang Rumanian songs in the little restaurant on the Eastside, while my mother smirked and the waiters with black mustaches stood against the walls, sucking their teeth.

There were the boys who wept because they had come so close but in the end had lost the championship, and others who wept because they had won it. There were army buddies, sitting in foxholes or barracks, holding the letter that said, "Forgive me, I'm going to marry Tim," while the tears slipped down their faces and they continued to hold the letter in front of them like a flower they were offering to the wind. They were hardly more than schoolboys, really, who years later, as fathers, hearing an old pop tune on the car radio as they drove their kids home from the movies, would remember that letter and weep again, hands gripping the steering wheel, not wiping the tears from their cheeks.

I've known men who sobbed when they remembered strolling hand in hand with their fathers through the cool of an evening in a garden or city park. They wondered why he had abandoned them, and searched for him all their lives, only to look in the mirror one morning, bleary-eyed and alone, to find that the face looking back at them was his.

And then there was the writer who wept whenever he read his stories to an audience. His mouth worked hopelessly around the words, the emotion blurring whatever he said. He had been famous when young, but fate and changing tastes had passed him by, although he wrote as well as ever. I thought he wept for the unrecognized beauty of his words. I was wrong.

2.

There are men who cry for their youth, or something they lost in it. Others weep in fear of old age, or for every moment that passes them by. But there are some, and I think the writer was one, who cry for others. I won't say these men have been sent among us to weep for us all, but they have come to an understanding that sees the end in all beginnings, and they mourn for the living, as well as the dead, before we and our world are gone.

These men are not indifferent to the world, or aloof. They do not spill their tears in condescending pity, but as an expression of suffering so personal it grabs their hearts like the hand of someone falling away from them on a mountainside.

I don't mean to suggest that I am one of this group, but recently tears have rolled from my eyes when I see the simplest things: lovers kissing on the street, workers waving placards on a picket line, a boy alone shooting baskets in a backyard, and all those teenagers who wear the same expressionless mask I discarded long ago.

3.

We can shout against the injustice and cruelty of other men, but how do we protest the elemental sufferings of loss and death? Like a moth beating against the window light, our anger must soften into a butterfly of mourning in the end.

That is the knowledge men have difficulty telling anyone. They spend a lifetime learning that to be human is to be a fulcrum balancing joy on one side and sorrow on the other, life on the palm of the right hand, death on the palm of the left—a wisdom so elemental they choose to remain silent in order to spare others, for a while at least, the knowledge we all must accept. And that may be why you sometimes see an old man—passing lovers on the street or boys shooting baskets in backyards—who suddenly, for no apparent reason, begins to weep.

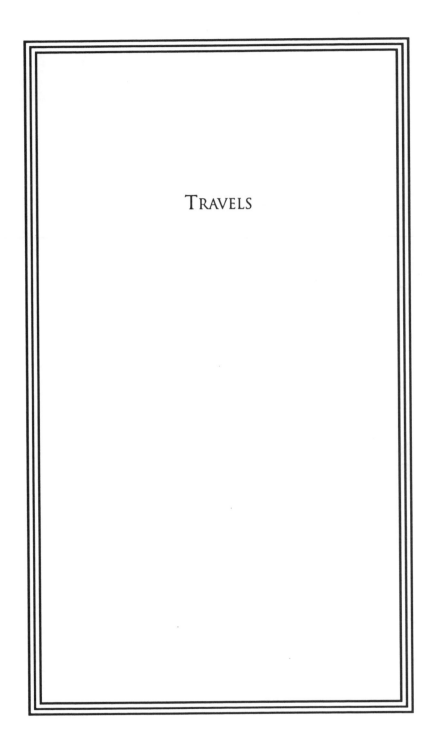

TRAVELS

JOURNEYS

Everything we undertake is a journey. Frying an egg, sipping a beer at a party, or making a bank deposit, we are on a journey as great as the ones undertaken to Troy, Mecca, Mt. Meru, or to Cathay along the old Silk Road.

We slide the egg from the pan to the plate, sit down and eat, then go about our chores, which may involve a "real" journey downtown or even across the seas.

But each event *is* a journey, nonetheless: The egg is a volcano that might have happened on the plate's plateau, and a landscape unfolds on the table beyond the plate. Although we are seated, we are on a journey across this landscape of crockery and glass, calling out to someone seated on the other side of the continent, someone we hope is there, waiting or making his or her way toward us.

If the chair opposite is empty, there is still the person at the party who has made his way toward us through a human forest, or who we approach through the same stand of talking trees.

We have debased so much. Consider the short trip across the teller's counter at the bank. Doesn't it resemble a confessional in church? The little gates are open, and the person on the other side is waiting to hear whatever you need to say.

TOURISTS

for Joe Stroud

In this land everything is poor. The people have pressed their backs into postures of humility and climb from crevices to beg for food.

We offered them coins, which they immediately ate, unaware of their teeth breaking. We offered them our scarves and hats, then our key chains, staring as they devoured each one.

Finally, we broke off slabs of rock, which some of them ate, while others began nibbling at our pant legs or running their wet tongues along the sleeves of our jackets.

We fed them our words, whole sentences, paragraphs, but still they kept eating. And when we turned, we found they had devoured our car, which lay on its side like the skeleton of a cow.

It was after they ate our clothes that the slimmest of us were able to escape: we ran naked among them and began wrenching up roots and desperately chewing.

Later we remembered that our passports had been in our pockets, and the guards at the border have refused us permission to pass.

Now we squat at the edge of the snow, waiting for tourists. But when they arrive, they only throw coins. We want to tell them who we are, and when no one is looking we attempt to grab their hands, which they hurriedly withdraw.

We have not lost hope, but we grow hungrier every day, and each of us has admitted than he can detect the odor of tourists for hours before they arrive.

In the City of Sunlight

I.

When strolling through the cobblestone streets with their nickel-plated gutters, one cannot help but observe the play of sunlight so peculiar to this city. Not only does the sunlight flutter from the nickel and from the chrome edges of the window frames, but it butterflies from the domes, bell towers and bridges, all made of platinum or polished pewter, and especially from the silver bells, where it sprawls in patches until they boom out the hour. Then it takes wing above the rooftops, a migration of butterflies dipping and soaring, darting in and out of streets, and fragmenting into a thousand other butterflies when it caroms off a platinum statue or the platinum canopy of a fountain in one of the city's hundred plazas. At such times, if one is a man turning a corner, he may see at the end of a shadowy arcade, or directly in front of him, a woman he half-remembers, turning away from him; and if one is a woman, she may encounter the slim-hipped man she has always dreamed of, pirouetting away from her like a ballet dancer.

Chalices full of jewels, glittering autos, glistening roasts—in short, anything wished for, anything desired (whether consciously or not) can be seen in the sunlight flittering from one metal object to the next. For this is the city where dreams are made palpable for a moment and then vanish, only to reappear for an instant in another courtyard, another platinum-fountained square.

It is unlikely that the founders intended these manifestations, since historically the city has been known for both its high incidence of suicide and its paucity of marriages. In truth, the city would have become a cemetery of silver-encrusted tombs centuries ago had not the youth of other nations made it into a resort.

II.

The young people come in spring, summer, and early autumn, when the city brims with sunlight almost daily; and they come in great numbers, most of them arriving alone or with friends they quickly abandon, hardly ever with parents or in couples. This migration has always been considered a curiosity, for no regularly scheduled airlines or ships serve the city, and only one train a week visits it. In addition, neither maps nor native guides can be found to direct one there, and in truth the city, a baroque ruin facing the ocean, is no longer inhabited. But that is why this city, with its crumbling walls overgrown with weeds, with its unkempt trees swaying ominously overhead, with its vines slithering onto the weed-cracked sidewalks, and with its piles of masonry gathered at the base of buildings or cluttering the nickelplated gutters—that is why this city is a city of the young.

III.

During the tourist season, one can see the youths dashing through the streets, arms outstretched, the males growling, the females gasping, as they attempt to catch the elusive sunlit phantoms. This is how they spend their days, falling exhausted at dusk and sleeping until dawn when they resume the pursuit. Sometimes two youths, chasing the same flitter of sunlight from different directions, will run into each other's arms; and sometimes, eyes glazed, they will remain holding on to each other for months, even years, their lips curved in a secret smile. These are the lucky ones.

The majority continue to bound after every sunlit bauble, pulling bricks from walls or searching among the masonry piled in the streets or wherever the sunlight seems to vanish. Few of the youths want to leave at vacation's end. Many stay. Some go mad and run off into the jungle. Others sit in the city's many abandoned doorways, hands open in their laps, and stare straight ahead: the fluttering sunlight continues to reflect on their irises, but their irises no longer move. And some realize that the butterflies would all disappear if the sunlight could no longer flutter off the metal, and individually or in groups they set to work polishing the domes and the towers, so that the metal has remained polished throughout the centuries although the city has decayed. A few even recognize that the phantoms are only a reflection of sunlight, yet even so they cannot give up their pursuit, and continue sprinting through the streets with increasingly haggard expressions.

IV.

The rains usually end all this. Winter here is a continuing torrent of silver shafts, all spearing straight into the heart of the city, which accepts them like a martyr. In this season, the faces of the young, pale and unshaven, their hair like grimy rags, can be seen in windows, looking out at the glistening city.

How they die is not important: suicide, heartbreak, the body just giving up. All winter long, their parents, journeying great distances, charter boats and planes, or struggle through the jungle on foot toward a location they do not know yet somehow remember. And almost always they arrive too late. These parents, who had encouraged their children's trip and bade them farewell the year before with such joy as they could hardly understand, return home so distorted with grief that their neighbors cannot bear to look at them, for the grief seems a double grief, as though the parents had somehow left their own lives in that vine-strangled city.

Before the parents return home, however, they bury their children in the jungle, so that by spring, when the sunlight begins its explosions of wings from the belfries and the first of the tourists enter its streets, the city is empty and quiet and seems to have been waiting all winter for the young people to arrive.

THE CULT OF THE BURNING FLOWERS

"...In the city's ancient fortresss, quarters were provided for those selected to perform atonement for the populace. These penitents, both male and female, were chosen at random from among the citizenry without regard to age, and were housed in dormitories set above the huge inner courtyard, just inside the western wall, the wall that faces the sea. This courtyard, really an enclosed grass field, was exposed to afternoon sunlight and surrounded by palm trees whose tops, rising above the battlements, could be seen from the center of the city.

"Each morning a priest, in a white robe and a headdress of flamingo feathers, entered the dormitories and announced the day's tasks. Ritual bathing was scheduled every two hours, beginning at sunrise and ending at 11 p.m. Ritual dressing occurred at 8 a.m., noon, 6 p.m., and 10 p.m. The hours between were assigned to long silences, fasts, scripture reading, or poking at one another's skins with needles until each participant seemed covered with berries.

"After a month of preparation, the acolytes, mutterimg hymns, would sway from the fortress, a procession of two hundred men and women in black robes, heads shaved, and proceed through the crowds gathered on the boulevards until they reached the palace garden, which the governor had turned into a public park. Here, wearing an elaborate robe made of peacock feathers and a silver-blue wig that fell in tiers to his shoulders, the governor would greet the acolytes in the name of the king. Then he would lead the procession, followed by the populace, back to the fortress, where the elders waited in the grassy courtyard, arranged in a circle around a pile of twigs, each holding aloft a burning torch and dressed in a scarlet robe open down the middle and a headdress topped with slender, sapphire-blue plumes that curled at the tips.

"The acolytes would surround the elders, and then one of the elders, without a signal, would step onto the twigs inside the circle of his peers, and, lighting the twigs with his torch, would be consumed in flames while standing erect, his torso so well-prepared over the years, through the continuous process of lancing and healing, that when his body blackened it would burst open and seem to gush forth a multitude of many-colored flowers before he fell.

"The achievement of this effect was all-important, and was thought to manifest a favorable disposition of the gods toward the city for the coming month, after which the next immolation would be performed. In time the penitents became known as 'The Cult of the Burning Flowers' and their acolytes as 'The Kindled Buds.' In fact, many words describing acts of penitence and horticulture are so interchangeable in their language that over the years they have caused scholars much confusion.

"At first, the position of the dormitories led historians to think that the fortress was a prison, with cellblocks open to the sea breeze on one side and the huge sunlit courtyard on the other, common architectural features found in their penal system today. But recently discovered documents make it clear that they were not prisons, that theft and homicide rarely occurred, and that the Cult of the Burning Flowers flourished with the people's consent and, indeed, their unswerving belief that those who sacrificed themselves were maintaining a moral and spiritual balance in the universe.

"Flowers were named for the martyrs, whose remains were buried on street corners throughout the city, and around whose graves small shaded parks were created by the populace, those same parks which lend the city its singular atmosphere, at once festive and pensive. This atmosphere has attracted tourists for uncounted years, most notably during the last weeks of April, when the city hosts an international horticultural convention. For two weeks, celebrations occur day and night, culminating on the final evening in the fortress's great inner courtyard, when the old men of the town, surrounded by their grandchildren, stumble in circles for hours on end, finally opening their shirts and tumbling forth a profusion of red and white camellias, as they fall to the ground in a drunken swoon."

LANGUEDOC

The town bakers have been dreaming while weevils prowl through the flour bins in their shops. In dozens of houses, children sleep the sleep of bliss, unaware of the doors of justice that open for some, close for others. Women, naked inside their nightgowns, resist the resentments that swarm through their sleep. They drift in the dark, holding torches high overhead, looking for tenderness among the rocks. Staggering through windy chasms, their men, lured away by thoughts of treasure or meeting God, turn toward home, empty-handed, unsure of the way back, their eyes no longer accustomed to the dark.

THE EXHIBITIONIST

There are days I want to eat my hair in public, on a busy street. It happens mornings, mostly, that this desire rises like a pressure of hot water forcing a passage through rock.

I stand among the breakfasting tourists with their guide books open to the Prince's palace and their conversation cumbersome with gilt-edged phrases. I stand before the waiters placing white cups of coffee on the tables and the birds singing in the sunlight, and tug a handful of hair from my head.

I won't pretend there isn't pain and not a small amount of blood. But my face shows none of this, and, with even the hint of a flourish, I place the clump unconcernedly in my mouth, much as an elephant removes his feeding of hay from the bale with his trunk and calmly buries it in his maw.

I chew, swallow, repeat the motion until my hair is gone and I stand bald and bloodied before them—ladies fainting, clasping guide books to their bosoms, while men fan them and complain of my country's moral turpitude. I stroll away.

Despite the pain, there is no experience so delicious in the morning. Even cigars after coffee do not contain the tang of that moment when I depart. Breezes billow in the banners hung like sails from the public buildings, the sun warms my skull, my brains glow, and the morning's light pours through my body.

I don't even mind the old women with their baskets of vegetables who point, whispering, "That's the one who eats his hair." Or, "I knew his mother, the whole family wasn't right." Nor the boys chalking the sidewalk in front of my house, or blowing whistles under my window after school.

I was annoyed only once, last year, when the city fathers told me that reports of my "performances" had increased the number of tourists who visited our town, and offered me an unending supply of toupees if I would eat my hair each day at a specific time and place.

I explained to them the torturous months of healing and how I nurtured each new growth of hair until it kept my skull in the dark, covered it like an eclipse, until the weight was too much, until I had to expose myself or subside into a pile of ashes filling a suit.

They nodded, renewed their offer, and appealed to my loyalty to the state. "Gentlemen," I said, "the answer is 'no.'" And walking from the room, I left it at that.

I haven't been bothered since. But their presumption still rankles whenever I recall it, for although I will admit that eating my hair concerns the tourists and has everything to do with the national character, it is in no way related to the commercial desires of shopkeepers or the economic sanctions of political men.

As for my "performances," they continue according to my own timetable, governed only by the sun and the wind and whatever sidereal map charts the ticking of the heavens inside my head.

SWALLOWS

I've seen them at sunrise and sunset in Greece, Italy, and California, dipping and swooping over the fields; skyfuls of them streaking this way and that, snatching up insects in mid-flight, but looking as if they are searching the earth for something lost or forgotten.

From a distance, a dozen or more resemble bits of paper thrown at the horizon. But they are never scattered by the wind: they slice through it, flitting over the stubble wherever they wish.

Wings arched like medieval bows, heads like arrows about to be launched, they wait on the frescoes of Minoan palaces and the enclosed walls of Egyptian tombs, buried for thousands of years in stone-stunned darkness, ready to take wing the instant a thief or scientist's torch flares into their night.

Keats and the others can have their nightingales. I'll take the swallows skittering from crumbling walls or bursting from tombs and twittering over fields everywhere on the planet: they are so much like words urgently waiting to be written, almost insisting they be chosen, as they snap up nuances too tiny to be seen, and seek their places on an empty page.

THE FACE

I was slick with sweat and panting from hillsides, and had knelt to drink from the sun-wrinkled surface of the River Usk, when I saw my face staring back at me from the sliding water.

The face was transparent, lidded by tree-shade and clouds going over, and the head behind it was hollow, filled with fish as fine as feathers and stones stuck in bottom mud.

Who was this, so clearly me surprised to come upon myself looking back into my face with a face that was as surprised as mine was?

It was me gone back to stones and mud, the self removed from the seeing eye, looking back at an observer who couldn't imagine what the other face beheld.

The river rolled and wrinkled by, but the face held fast, as if staring from behind a window. It was imprisoned by my watching it, as I was imprisoned by its watching me.

I stared, and it stared back. Then I bent to the water and kissed as much as drank the face, and the water channeled through me, a branching coldness like the fingers of a hand reaching out and holding on.

Even before I rose, I knew the water's surface would splinter and shake and reform into the sliding river, sun-wrinkled and expressionless once again.

I make no claim beyond the telling. I left that place no wiser than before, but carrying a second self who has swayed within me ever since—silent, self-contained, waiting beneath every breath I draw.

My Encounter With the Eternal Mystery

I encountered the Eternal Mystery once. It was on a spring night in Zagreb several years ago, in the unlighted hallway of a musty walk-up where I'd gone to visit the acquaintance of a friend, a narrow hallway where the odors of vinegar and coal gas had settled permanently in the darkness. I hadn't taken ten steps into that darkness when I became aware of a hulking presence facing me from the depths of the hall. "Excuse me," I said automatically to the figure, and waited for a reply, my body tense, poised for whatever might happen. The figure didn't answer. "Excuse me," I repeated, a quaver in my voice. Again there was no reply. I held my breath and listened, my heartbeat resounding from the walls, but I heard nothing, and it was so dark I couldn't find the number of the apartment door I was looking for as a possible escape. "Excuse me?" I said again, taking a tentative step forward, but whoever or whatever was in that hall with me remained silent, advancing toward me with each step I took toward it. I stopped and listened again, straining to see that other figure, and when I resumed my steps my nerves were so jangled I didn't know whether I was advancing farther into the hall or returning the way I had come. I stopped again and stood with the darkness surrounding me, and listened to my breathing, hoping to hear the breathing of the other, but there was only the darkness pressing in on me as if someone had flung a heavy cloak around my soul. I began to tremble. "Excuse me," I said for the fourth time, the words sounding more like a prayer than the apologies of an intruder or a clumsy tourist. What else could I have done—drop to my knees like a child at the side of a bed and, with hands joined, breathlessly ask a being who lives in the dark to protect Mommy and Daddy and especially me from the scaly, fire-eyed creature who, at that moment, I may have been praying to? No: that idea alone made me firm my stance, even though I was still trembling, sweat smearing my body as if I'd been anointed. "I said, 'Excuse me!'" I repeated once again, but this time louder, with a twinge of annoyance in my voice at not being answered, and the defiance in my tone unexpectedly thrilled me. The breath seethed from between my clenched teeth. Simultaneously I heard, or thought I heard, a muffled snort or growl. It was a gagging sound, a struggle for breath that mimicked my own and, almost instantly, dissolved my annoyance, so clear was its desire to communicate, and so clear was its inability to do so, as if its words were trapped inside a muzzled snout. Understand, the entire incident had taken no more than several moments, and as I strained to interpret the gasping of that other, I had the strongest impression yet that someone stood facing me. At that instant a blade of light sliced through the dark from a wrenched-open door and a silhouetted figure bellowed in Croatian, "What's all the noise? What do you want?" The light gave me my bearings, and without a word I turned and ran from the building.

When I returned the next morning, I was surprised to find how short the hallway was. In the gray daylight, I could see a staircase to my left, and set against the wall beneath it a narrow table topped with envelopes and circulars and a small vase with wilted flowers. There was no other furniture, except a full-length mirror beyond the table at the end of the corridor, placed there, I assume, to make the hall look longer. I watched myself advancing toward it, an anonymous figure with the light at its back, looming larger with each step, and I muttered, almost involuntarily, "I am who I am."

STEP ON A CRACK, BREAK YOUR BACK

(A Heroic Tale of the City By Joseph Conrad,
found, compiled, and edited by Morton Marcus)

Marlowe was speaking:

"The decision can only be made when one is in bed just over-coming an illness, or in a small pub at night with swirling red and green lights revolving over the till. 'I'll do it!' you say, smacking the table. 'By God, I'll do it!'

"All your life, it seems, has ferried you to this moment, has pre-pared you for this event: your nation's history, your education—all to do this one thing: STEP ON A CRACK IN THE SIDEWALK, AND DAMN THE RESULTS, whether they be to break your back, break wind, or brake the hansom cab to a stop! And you stride into the street where the cracks hide their destinies in crooked shadows slithering through the pavement....

"So it was with me. With such resolve, I had hoisted myself from bed—where I had been convalescing from a recurrent illness I acquired several years before on a voyage to Malaya—and found myself in front of my house. The banners on the balconies above me seemed to flout the heavens, and the sunny afternoon sidewalk stretched before me like a minefield.

"I waded into it, hopping between cracks as I always do, count-ing them:
>   'One, two,
>   Buckle my shoe.
>   Three, four—'

"But it was different today. Today I was playing a different game. Today it was only a matter of time before I chose the most treach-erous crack on which to place my shoe and lean down with my whole weight, crushing the crack and all its legend like a snake—

"And there it was! A leering black mouth on the pavement!

"I went to bridge the crack with my shoe before pressing down, but suddenly the crack yawned open and my foot fell into it, and then my whole leg was dragging me down, and before I could draw back, I had fallen into what was now a chasm closing around me.

"Luckily, my hands had caught on the sidewalk on either side of the crack and were now braced flat, supporting my whole body, which swung helplessly below in the hot fissure.

"Immediately, my shoulders began to ache, and even before the surprising events had a chance to settle in my mind, I was hoisting myself up on my palms, like a novice on the parallel bars.

"My torso rose above the crack: the sidewalk was now a rolling plain, spongy and moist beneath my palms. Simultaneously, I saw myself as if from a great height, struggling from the fissure, and I realized I was watching myself haul my body up from the life line in the palm of my left hand. Meanwhile, the one who was hoisting himself up was watching while a smaller self hoisted himself from the life line in his hand, while that one watched yet another who was struggling to rise from his.

"That was all I could see. But once I had scrambled from the fissure and lay panting by its side, I had a sense that all my movements were being mimicked by an infinity of smaller movements. And when I raised my arms, a gale sweeping down upon my head told me that my motions were being duplicated by a larger self yet.

"This sense of simultaneous selves has continued to haunt me in all I do. It is the legacy of my adventure. Even speaking these words, these words, these words within, these words within words....

"We live in such a world, my friends. Ah, well, let us drink up, and not let this knowledge break our backs."

(1919)

148

Invitation to the Metaphysician's Cottage

So this is what happens when one is invited to supper at the metaphysician's cottage—here at the end of the lane overlooking the entire valley, which, when we entered, was visible in the last of the day's chilly light. I remember smoke shawling upward from the farmers' huts and swaying toward us. The odors of woodsmoke and oregano and hides drifted on the air, as did the mournful hymn sung by the choir of motherless children in the village church. On top of the mountain opposite, the outline of a ruined castle was a jagged memory against the brass-colored sky.

Last night we sat in a farmer's hut, smelling the hams hung from the shadowy crossbeams as we listened to the old men, their faces flickering in the firelight, discuss the price of barley and annual yields, and tell stories of half-remembered landlords whose fortunes were lost in shipwrecks, and of lovers who missed each other by moments on mountain paths that would have led them to safety and long lives. There were stories of children maimed from birth, parents killed in threshing accidents, and fathers gone berserk who butchered their families. Afterwards, we sat staring at the fire. The silence was unbearable.

We had not expected to stay more than a night in this district, but then today we received the metaphysician's invitation, and since we are visiting this country as a cultural delegation we could not decently refuse.

Besides, they are an extraordinary bunch, these metaphysicians. They can be seen until the first snow, strolling in groups through the cities or in the countryside, their purple robes gathered decorously around them, as they discuss every conceivable subject. At times they picnic in quiet plazas or under the huge oak trees that border the plowed fields. On such occasions, shopkeepers, plumbers, field workers, and anyone else around may join them, sharing their lunches and listening to the conversation. At times great festivals have resulted from such modest beginnings, and in several instances we observed crowds gather by the thousands around these conversations as around tournaments: children dashing back and forth, shrieking and laughing, their parents passing food and drink around, and all creating such a hubbub that it was impossible to hear what the wisemen were saying. Through it all, the metaphysicians seemed unconcerned and continued their discussion.

In truth, the people love the metaphysicians and bring them food and flowers and clean their homes. In fact, the entire community provides housing for them, and even the smallest children will proudly announce the name of the metaphysician living in their town.

That is why we entered the metaphysician's wisteria-covered doorway with such enthusiasm. Inside, a smoky fire provided the only light, and a cinnamon-like incense burned our eyes. The metaphysician sat in the midst of his protégés, a huge hippopotamus of a man in a golden gown, wearing a square brimless black cap clamped on his head, the golden emblem of an all-seeing eye embroidered on its front. He stared at us with bulging eyes as his protégés fluttered and capered around him. They questioned us for hours over local brandy and cigars, and we watched their shadows bow and swirl in the firelight as they calculated and measured our opinions before entering them in a large book with an ivory clasp, after forcing us to define every nuance of every word we used, no matter how vehemently we insisted that we only half-comprehended their language. All the while, they bickered among themselves over terminology, and when their babbling became too uproarious, the metaphysician would raise his hand for quiet and, never taking his eyes from ours, would intone a phrase or sentence that would make his followers murmur and nod. In one such sentence he proclaimed, "A cause is the effect of a previous cause, since that cause was induced by consequences of a previous effect."

"What about the lovers who could have met on a mountain path?" I finally asked. "And what about the children maimed from birth?"

He licked his lips and replied, "All action is a matter of will. This principle can be traced to the prime mover, who acted in creating the world only after he had willed this action, thereby establishing a pattern for all finite eternity."

He ended the evening by saying that it was man's duty to experience the endless present as rationally as possible.

"Unfortunately," he added, "man can only contemplate the present after it has passed, like a street he has ridden by and doesn't quite remember and therefore at best can only approximate as far as its dimensions are concerned, or its situation in the town, or whether he has really passed by it at all." In fact, he and his protégés seemed obsessed with defining this "endless present," and determining whether we (and for that matter they) were really sitting in the cottage discussing these subjects at all.

That is how we come to be standing here now, just outside the metaphysician's door, most of us nauseated and sweaty. The night is clear and cold. The stars, like pieces of glass embedded in the darkness, glitter down on us and seem to grind into our heads. We can no longer see the valley or the wisteria-covered door—but listen! You can still hear the racket coming from the cottage—that bickering and babbling, and the metaphysician's voice trumpeting over all.

Last night, one of the old farmers told us with a wink that this noise was the reason the metaphysician had been given the cottage at the end of the lane. But the ploy had not been successful, for on clear nights, the old man confided, you could hear the voices of the metaphysician and his protégés the length of the valley. However, he admitted, nodding his head, the voices gave him a sense of comfort when he settled to sleep beneath his quilt and sensed the huge darkness expanding outward from around his hut. "You see," he said, "even though they sound like dogs yelping at the moon, they keep us from forgetting."

"Forgetting?"

"Yes. If the metaphysicians did not exhort us to contemplate an endless present, we would forget the ridge, the ruined castle, even the orphans in the church. As with a religious ritual, we know the duties of our daily lives so well we no longer remember what they are, even as we perform them, and, in truth, we would forget the metaphysicians' words if their outlandish quibbling and costumes did not demand our attention."

"And would you forget your suffering as well?"

"In a way, yes," the old man said. "Sometimes we are so oppressed by our suffering that we think it is the natural state of our existence. But merely by their presence, the metaphysicians give the lie to that."

THE BELL AT THE BOTTOM OF THE SEA

More than a hundred men in a merchant galley were carrying a church bell from Constantinople to Venice in 1330 or thereabouts when a storm swirled up in the Adriatic several hundred miles from their destination. The ship listed left and right, the bell strained in its harness, and the captain, seeing no other way, ordered the bell pushed overboard. It sank, a giant's thimble, in a moment. The sailors said they could hear it tolling as it plunged to the bottom, a grumbling sound—as if a god, clearing his throat, were about to proclaim "salvation," said some; "apocalypse," said others. Since that day, many have reported hearing the bell—this bell now universally known as *La Campana al Fondo del Mare*, "The Bell at the Bottom of the Sea"—and many have tried to describe the peculiar sound of its tolling, muffled by water and padded by centuries of accumulated algae, all imagining a religious ceremony being called hundreds of fathoms below their keel, as if they sailed over a drowned village where the bell in a church steeple continued to summon worshippers to Angelus, and to all the other holy hours of the year.

"There! You hear it?" asked the mate, after telling me the story. His index finger was raised as if to silence talk or mark a beloved passage of music, a smile of satisfaction on his lips.

I shook my head.

"Listen!" he insisted, wetting his lips with his tongue, his finger still raised.

I shook my head again, realizing he wasn't paying attention to me, and hadn't, really, been talking to me from the beginning. He didn't need me or anyone else to corroborate what he already knew. The story and his invitation to join him in listening for the bell were part of a ritual he and other sailors observed every time they crossed this point in their voyage.

It was also clear that the observance of the ritual was more important than actually hearing the bell, and that keeping the story alive from one century to the next was of more consequence than either, a connection between worlds that in the end would lead to a satisfactory, if not joyous, conclusion for all who believed in the story.

"There," he said, his lips quivering. "You hear it?"

I shook my head once more and walked away, feeling neither superiority nor annoyance, but I was disturbed, extremely disturbed, aware as never before that the heart sunk in my chest was surrounded by a silent sea.

VACATION

On vacation in a foreign city, we find that all the newspapers are printed in a language we do not understand. When we open each one, the pages unfurl like schooner sails, and we stare dumbfounded at the gibberish arranged in orderly, meaningless columns.

The newspaper billows and fills as we open it full-length in our search for news from home, then it hoists us unexpectedly into the air as if we were hang gliders, sailing us into countrysides where we recognize neither the roads nor the slant of the farmhouse roofs below.

It's then we relax, realizing that this was what we wanted all along—to go where nothing would be familiar, where the roads sliding up and down hills would lead us to a sense of ourselves we had never known before—free of falling prices, riots in the streets, and family obligations.

We sail over the landscape, buoyed by warm breezes, our arms feeling neither the weight of the newspaper above nor the pull of our body below, as we drift languidly, lazily, dreamily over forests and lakes,

until a flapping overhead turns our gaze upward and we find the black columns of print rearranging themselves on the newspaper, which is suddenly heavy, sodden with weight, causing it to lose altitude and descend toward a burning village where we see the running figures before we hear the gunshots and the screams.

THE 8TH, 9TH, AND 10TH
WONDERS OF THE WORLD

In the midst of a civil war, two men were arrested in different sections of the same city and summarily sentenced to be executed the next morning.

One of the men had been a spy and blown up a barracks, killing twenty soldiers. The other had done nothing, but his protestations of innocence had gone unheeded by his captors.

Both men spent their last night in the same cell. The cell, which had been the basement of a family home before the war, smelled of urine and goats. It contained no lights and no furniture, and the two men sat in the dark on the straw-strewn stone floor, exchanging small talk about their lives and listening to the howitzers thumping on the hills above the city and the small arms fire occasionally stuttering through the streets.

Suddenly the spy blurted out with a bitter laugh, "They say there are seven wonders of the world—the Hanging Gardens at Babylon, the Lighthouse at Pharos, the Great Wall of China. But these are all things men have built, physical things, and almost every one of them has disappeared like dust in the wind, as we will tomorrow.

"I tell you this: there is an eighth wonder, my friend, and it is the human imagination. We can conceive of anything—not just those seven constructions, but a warm willing woman who will love us when we are lonely, a good meal when we are hungry, and a successful end to this war, when we will finally be at peace and our people in power.

"That is what keeps me going and that is why I blew up the barracks—and that is why I am not afraid to die."

His voice shivered away in the darkness.

The innocent man shifted on the straw but didn't reply. His face was covered with shadows and the spy couldn't see his expression.

156

They sat in silence for several minutes. Then the innocent man began to speak with great difficulty in a small voice, as if struggling to find the words for his thoughts. "I don't know. I was thinking as you spoke that there had to be something beyond the imagination. I'm not sure, but maybe it is the fact that somewhere along the line those who have taken me from my wife and children and condemned me to die will be forgiven.

"If I cannot forgive them, maybe my wife will, or my children, or my children's children. I mean, hatred cannot go on forever.

"And when it occurred to me just now that all of us contain this capacity to forgive, I said to myself, 'If the imagination is the eighth wonder of the world, surely forgiveness is the ninth.'"

"I'll agree to that," exclaimed the spy with a snicker, "if you'll agree that the tenth wonder is our capacity to forget."

The Tale of a Doorknob

A lieutenant salutes his major, nods to an enlisted man who triggers a heavy artillery piece. Five miles away, a child hugging a rag doll closes an apartment door behind her as the door, apartment, whole building collapses before she can remove her hand from the knob. She will be found that way in the rubble, gripping the round piece of metal she had turned in the door countless times on the mornings she went out to play or run to the store for her mother—overcast mornings, sunny mornings, mornings filled with rain.

The soldiers will wonder at the little girl without a face who lies ten feet away from the remains of a rag doll, still holding a round metal object that looks like a doorknob. Several of them will stare, several others will turn away or throw up or curse the hills, the enemy, the war, even the perfidy of humankind. Invaders or defenders, their reactions will be the same.

Only two or three—a general, a sergeant, a private—will be struck by the thought that the girl is holding what could be a globe of the world, or some other symbolic shape, and one of them will gently, or not so gently, pry her fingers open to retrieve the object and bring it home to his children as a souvenir, accompanying the gift with tales of conquest in a foreign country, or with instructions for merciless vengeance in his own land.

TEARS

As the child in the doctor's waiting room struggled against his mother's grip, flinging his head from side to side and wailing because he couldn't get his way, one of his tears sailed off into the shadows—a slightly flattened droplet glinting for a moment in the sunlight tumbling through the window—an oblong, wobbling weight of translucent light, like a planet slipping into an astronomer's lens for an instant and then disappearing.

All those tears released in anger, sorrow, joy, frustration, fear; in pain, relief, anxiety, envy, despair—every day they wing off into shadows and darkened corners, and every night they return as the stars that guide us across the deserts of sleep.

THE ARMIES ENCAMPED IN THE FIELDS
BEYOND THE UNFINISHED AVENUES

"It is absurd to resist what cannot be resisted," we said, and hung the banners from every window. We did not know how arrogant the strangers would be. "Learn to accept the unacceptable and you will survive," they said, and began organizing us into labor gangs.

Their first decree announced that the avenues would not be finished, and we knew that all absences were permanent, that our hands were to remain open like the cisterns in the ruins beyond the city, where flies crawled back and forth on the dry clay.

In the manner of their speech, "absence" became the word we used to delineate those places where the avenues went unfinished, and "absence" also came to describe the ocean, where all roads end. The dog without a leash was no longer called "freedom" but "separation" and "rupture," for we now saw it tottering from garbage can to garbage can in the alleys, eaten by flies that fed on its mouth. Night, and the rooster who ended it, we simply called "sky," enunciating the firmament's changing hues with many synonyms, from "everlasting absence" and "cosmic separation" to "eternal rupture."

But soon we were faced with an unsettling incoherence: An old man, addressed by the new expression for "good morning," crumbled to dust. A widow, calling her son to supper in a recently revised phrase of endearment, was ripped apart by a pack of wild dogs. And during the last election, mobs of voters, thinking they were obeying the new voting instructions, crowed the names of their choices like drunken choirs as they jigged and curtsied around the polling places. After this incident—a situation the strangers would not tolerate—plans for future elections were canceled, and whole neighborhoods were trucked into the desert, never to be heard from again.

The new language was with us in our bedrooms and kitchens, as if it had been assigned to live with us for the duration, always foreign but always there, until each of us seemed to be occupied by a second self, or more accurately by two people, one whose presence we took for granted, and the other whom we watched in terrified fascination, like a husband or wife you realize one day you have never really known.

The rubble piled up: scraps of old letters, broken plastic clocks, buttons and old batteries, rusted springs. War was imminent, the strangers announced, which was a surprise to most of us, since we thought that war was what we were engaged in already.

What would have happened had not the janitor discovered the armies encamped in the fields beyond the unfinished avenues is pure conjecture. But children were already stopping on the street and for no reason hauling down their britches and shouting words at passers-by that no one could understand.

"Where are you going? Back to your homes!" blared the loudspeakers on the trucks. "There is nothing there: no army! no fields! Absence exists beyond the avenues! Absence, separation—only that!"

Some turned back, but most of the crowd continued on, and we heard the murmurs from the people in front spreading back to us like the sounds of a distant ocean, until all of us stood beyond the concrete pilings of the unfinished avenues, laughing, applauding, crying, and pointing at the field beyond, where the soldiers, whose uniforms we did not recognize and who did not notice us, seemed to caper as they went about their chores, singing the old songs of love and death in a dialect that was used before we were born, while their red, violet, and yellow caps bobbed in the sunlit breeze.

"I Could Hear the Shouting"

I could hear the shouting from the stadium. It came in waves, in rhythmic murmurs rising to ragged crescendoes. The square outside was empty. It was that hour: the sun searing the cobblestones, the shops closed.

Only one store was open, and a heavyset man stood in the doorway, covered to the knees by a white apron smeared with rusty blood. Next to him, an old-fashioned red enamelled bin, full of soda bottles, proclaimed *Coca-Cola* in a flowing white script. I reached into its dark waters and lifted an icy bottle by the neck. It emerged like a jeweled fish. "Hot day for soccer," I said

The man in the apron sucked his teeth. "No soccer: *politika*," he muttered, pushing his chin toward the stadium across the square. I followed his gaze. No one was outside, but as I turned a roar rose from its roofless depths.

"Again *politika*. Crazy in the brain. All of them," the man said, and when I turned back to him, he was shambling into the shadowy interior of the shop, shaking his head.

I followed with the bottle cold in my hand, fumbling for change, engulfed by earth smells—oregano, thyme, loam-sprouted mushrooms and artichokes. The shop was like an unlit cave, and my eyes had trouble adjusting to the dark.

I had come into that city on my way to another, hitchhiking through a landscape of forests bordered by burnt-out villages and scorched by patches of charred trees.

The man in the apron stood at a block of wood behind a glass case in the rear of the shop. He had picked up a cleaver and was hacking at a side of meat. He stopped and pointed the cleaver at me. "My son go. I say 'No.' He go anyway. All of them. Never change."

Then he resumed rhythmically chopping the meat, his stroke steady as a heartbeat.

"Never change," he repeated with a sigh, a tiredness, an inevitability in his voice, as the cleaver continued to rise and fall. And for a moment he appeared to be presiding over the event at the stadium, like a judge firmly but resignedly hammering his gavel for order, knowing that no one was paying him the slightest attention.

DOING IT TO OTHERS

for Naomi Shihab Nye

In Croatia, where I've just been, the Serbs really did it to the poor Croatian farmers, my truly wonderful in-laws. But every moment I was there, I was aware that the Croats had done it to the Serbs, Jews, and Gypsies five decades before, and the Jews did it to the Palestinians afterwards, and the Gypsies are doing it to everyone, and everyone is doing it to everyone else; and I wondered where that left me—on one hand, a poet singing about the joys of being human and alive, and on the other, the child of immigrants who like everyone else distrusted, feared, or hated anyone not like themselves.

I know that whoever I am is carrying my ancestors' distrusts and hatreds wherever I go, as well as their longings for an end to suffering and injustice, and as a poet I am expressing both the hatreds and the longings from a deep place, or rather my ancestors and my people—dispossessed or dispossessing—are speaking them through me, as yours are through you, and we have little choice but to let them do so, even though we know that whoever our people are they'll probably do bad things to others when they get the chance.

But I still believe that when we get that chance, you and I can change everything, for then our peoples' hatreds will be as much our personal possessions as they ever will—together with the longings for an end to injustice and victimization—and we can choose to merge the hatreds with the longings so they will become reminders that whoever we are we were once the sufferers and should now remember that and open our fists and reach out our fingers to others, as if our fingers are magic wands that can transform the world.

MEMORY

In Denmark a few years ago, I met a professor Martens or Martensen—I can't remember which—who told me that memories could mollify our passions and soothe our restlessness and fears.

He theorized that through memory we enclosed the past, that we remembered everything, and he agreed with Jung that we could even recall seminal memories of our nation, tribe, and species.

"The past is anchored, locked in place, and therefore gives us security, even if the clarity of the incidents fade or become confused as we grow older," he said, and continued with a smile: "Memory allows us to face the uncertainties of the future with the confidence of knowing that at least 'our backs are covered,' as you Americans say."

Many times since that conversation I have imagined my memories late at night, herded in the corral outside the house. They are dark shapes shifting from leg to leg, snuffling and scratching the hoof-scarred earth, bristly rumps and snouts nudging one another as they mill about.

Then the scream. There is always the scream from the wooded hills a mile or so across the valley, and it is never clear if the scream is from a woman or a mountain lion.

Whatever the noise, the animals in the corral begin to twitch and mutter, turning this way and that, butting and pawing.

At the first scream I come to the bedroom window and look down, smelling the sweat-lathered hides. They writhe below me, shadows with heft and substance. I say to myself, "They are remembering, or being remembered," just as the scream sounds again, closer now, a jagged noise that makes the herd groan and stamp in a more agitated movement that I understand is the signal for me to do something.

At this point I remember that this scene has occurred many times before, and will happen many times again, and each time I experience the sensation that there is something I must do that is vitally necessary in the scheme of things, but I can never remember what it is.

As at those other times, I'm left peering at the landscape for a lumbering form, sweating myself now, not knowing if what I'm looking for is human or animal, wounded or healthy, and whether it shrieks in pain or is announcing its murderous presence.

The Storyteller

for Eduardo Galeano

In the town there was a storyteller, an old man who told outrageous stories about brooms that were girls in swinging skirts and giants who were snoring volcanoes.

Not only did he tell the stories, he was in them, either dancing so lustily with the girls in their crinkly skirts that they knew they were beautiful, even if they weren't; or placing a pond like a cup of water near the volcano, so the sleeping giant wouldn't wake with a parched throat and smother the village below with his fiery breath.

The old man told stories about how bars of soap, when rubbed diligently between the hands, turned into fish and swam around the sink, and how napkins, when folded the proper way, would fly around the dining room after every meal.

All his stories were impossible but never cruel, even when he told about spanking the cat because it ate the goldfish that was, in reality, his wife, who had died of the flu fifty years before, or slapping his nephew because the boy had swept out the fireplace without crossing himself, not knowing that the ashes were the remains of the dead and should always be treated with respect.

The children crowded around the old man on street corners after school, or in the shadowy arcade near the marketplace on weekends. Their parents never objected to the old man and his stories, no matter how impossible the stories were, nor did they tell the children they were wasting their time by listening to him.

After he finished telling a story, the old man would sit back and smile, and the children would press around him and whisper their fears and wishes into his ears. And the next week, or even the next day, those secrets would miraculously appear in one of the old man's tales.

The old man's stories were told and retold everywhere in the town. He told them for more than forty years, and the children grew and told them to their own children and continued telling them after the old man died.

This happened in another country and may not be true. It was told to me by a student whose name I have forgotten. He said he knew the old man when he was a boy and had seen the soap swimming and the napkins flying and could see them now. He said that the old man had begun telling the stories five years after his wife's death, and that he had never remarried and never had children.

The student believed that by telling his stories the old man imagined he had made the town children his own. I disagree. More likely the old man considered the stories to be his children, and he was sending them out to play with the other children in the streets and alleys near the marketplace. In this way, he populated the town with his offspring, and with every change the stories underwent on other tongues, with every shift of tone and nuance, with every added detail, they became his children's children, dressed in the latest fashion maybe, but preserving an essential family resemblance beneath their clothes.

I envied the old man his stories as I envied the student and the others who heard them and believed them enough to let them take on a life of their own. I knew that in time the stories could become more real than the town and its inhabitants, especially if the townspeople, like my student, traveled to different places in the world and told them to the people they met.

Because of what the student told me, a little of the old man and his town resides in me now, even though I have forgotten the student's name and never knew the old man's name or the name of the town. Again, the stories may not be true. The student was something of a smirker, as I remember, and could well have fabricated the old man, the tales, and the town itself to impress the ears of a willing teacher who saw less and less in the world to marvel at. If so, he only fooled himself, for he created a place that exists, as all such places do, beyond the wind that will continue after he and I are gone—the wind that whips sunlight and shadows before it, as it hurtles through abandoned villages and silent ruins.

Moon & Flower

for Djuro Radović

Moon and flower: a lilting breeze, the pale, reflected moonlight washing over the stone flower.

My wife and I went there, high up, thousands of feet over the bare mountains into sun-parched uplands all limestone and under-brush: white, gray, sand-colored rocks, and the tough shrubs grip-ping down, the dusty bushes, the dry creepers and spiraling cypress trees—stunted, crippled shapes holding fast year after year against sun and wind: so high and otherworldly, my mind swam beyond the precipices of time and space.

And finally—over stone roads, lanes really, immemorial tracks winding past forgotten walls of piled rock and occasional farms holding on as stubbornly as the vegetation around them—we arrived at this wind-lashed cemetery where stone grave-lids, ten-foot long rectangular slabs, were scattered about like lichen-spotted dominoes the gods had played with and abandoned eons before.

In one corner, past brambles and briars, stood a gray stone five feet across and six feet high, its front and back surfaces carved with lines of skirted figures dancing arm in arm among birds and hors-es and other half-formed animals, its narrow sides incised with strange hieroglyphs on one end, and on the other a crescent moon rising over a stone flower.

No one is sure who placed the stone there a thousand years ago or more, carved the indecipherable words, and chiseled the child-like figures who century after century have continued to perform their jubilant dance.

"Moon and flower," said Djuro, the friend who drove us there, pointing to the stone and then to the scattered grave-lids. "Look on new grave here: one grave, two grave, all—you see? Is symbol now—moon and flower—everywhere in valley."

170

"Moon and flower," my wife murmured, the people long settled in this place—family we'd come to visit—as much her people as Djuro's. "Moon and flower," she repeated. "What does it mean?"

"No one know. People come—my peoples, yours—and see and make it symbol. A mystery. These peoples long gone, finished," and he brushed his palms together as if ridding them of dust.

My peoples. The way he said it—the set of his jaw, the pride in his voice—the three of us understood he was not only referring to the inhabitants of those mountains and the valley we'd driven from, but also to their doggedly rebuilding this land after the third foreign invasion in less than a hundred years.

But why the moon and flower? Did these people recognize in it a forgotten ancestral memory that triggered an urge in them to resurrect it as a symbol, or was it merely the suggested softness of the flower that attracted them, the gentle illumination of the moon, the evocation I had just heard in my wife's voice of peaceful evenings that all of us in one way or another hope to secure?

Tonight, quiet, having contemplated all evening the ends of empire—palaces and skyscrapers toppling over the precipice of time—and having been moved to melancholy by the moonlight beyond the window, I thought of the standing stone high in the moonlight of that other place thousands of miles away, and imagined a breeze slipping over the crescent moon and the stone flower and then passing over the skirted figures, who in their place on top of the world, night after night, year after year, their movements open only to the gaze of the blind universe, continue to dance.

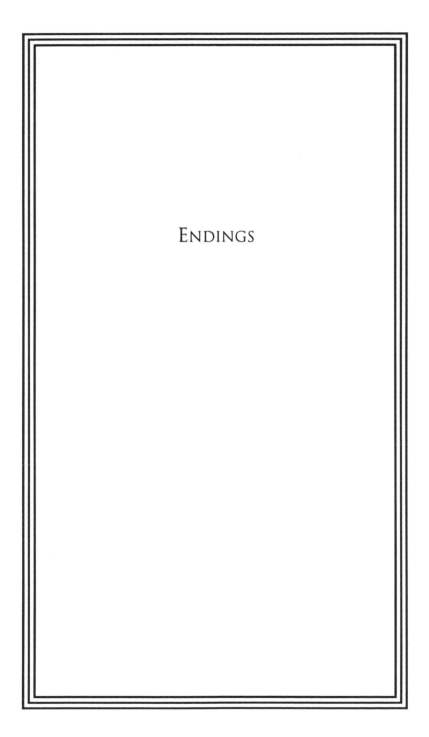

ENDINGS

GOODBYE TO THE TWENTIETH CENTURY

Goodbye, Mother. Don't feel guilty. You didn't let us down; we let you down. You existed only for us, and we responded to your pampering and protectiveness by destroying almost everything that came within our grasp. And now with few regrets, most of us turn our backs on you and leave you behind.

You had such hopes, such ambitions for us, and we disappointed you. Now you sit, a palsied old woman hunched in the corner of the kitchen, hardly more than a large shadow hovering on the wall, watching us, it must seem, celebrating your death, behaving like children concerned only with the party ahead, as we continually glance at the door on the day we finally leave home.

Don't be despondent. At the stroke of midnight, the house won't become a pumpkin rotting in a field. The instant the tower clock tolls twelve, the house will transform into a museum, which will carry in its depths the mementos and bric-a-brac of the century, like those children's rooms that mothers keep exactly as they were before the children left home for good.

And what a museum it will be—large enough to house biplanes with canvas wings, zeppelins and B-17s, jet fighters and rockets, and a complete collection of antique cars. Entire wings of the museum will be devoted to fashions in clothes and hairdos, and others to all sorts of weaponry. Exhibition halls will be dedicated to toys and games, portrait galleries to photographs of prime ministers and athletes and movie stars, and room after room to instruments of torture and to dioramas of plaster animals posed among exotic trees, all now extinct. Many of the exhibits will be painful reminders, to be sure—but at least some of your children and grandchildren will come to visit on weekends and rainy days.

And of those visitors, some, perhaps, will be curious, and stroll thoughtfully from room to room, and maybe they will come upon the chamber that sits in the center of the museum, surrounded by all the other rooms and connecting halls, like a throne room in the middle of a maze. You know the room, the one that glows in the darkness and is filled with display cases stretching into the shadows on all sides. Each case contains not butterflies but dreams in many shapes and hues, iridescent pinks and golds and blues that retain their brilliance and seem to wait in breathless slumber, as if they would take wing at the slightest prodding, flying from those glass cases that every hundred years are transported from the depths of one museum to another.

INTO THE NEW MILLENNIUM

Like a surfer expecting the years will build to a wave and the wave will crest into the next century, I feel the long pull of time catapult me toward shore on my coffin-lid board, forcing me to walk my individual plank with the weight of history, like a pirate ship, behind me.

Is it rapture, giddiness, or fear I feel as I swerve one way and another under the stars, keeping the difficult balance needed in such uncertain footing while I'm swept toward shore?

I'm a supple croucher, taking the wave as it comes and abandoning it before it splinters against the beach like a foundering ship full of useless cargo. By then, I'm paddling toward the next wave, still a hill, a ton of water that will never know it's a wave when it becomes one, nor that it's the wreckage of the wave that came before it.

Funny, but the shoreline is never the object; the ride is. Ask any surfer worth the salt he swishes through. The best of them don't look forward or back, and so cannot turn into pillars of even their own communities, whether or not they remain stationary on their rushing boards.

It's the rhythm, finally, that enthralls. The board points its finger, and I follow.

THE LIGHT WAS OUT

I kissed her in the hallway. The light was out. We fumbled with each other in the darkness at the bottom of the stairs, and our breath was more like hissing than lovers' murmurings. She didn't love me, and I didn't love her. I thought it then, and wasn't half surprised when she broke away and stood shuddering in the shadows, turned from me. "No," she said, "they'll hear." She'd said that the other time, and the time before that, when the light was on, and I imagined them, old and in bathrobes, coming to the stairhead, looking down on us and calling, "Ellie, is that you?" But now the light was out and there was no excuse. "Come on," I said, and reached for her because I thought I should, although I knew it was no use. "No!" It was as final as goodbye, and was.

I never saw her after that, but heard from time to time that she had married and divorced and married once again, that she'd had a daughter by her first husband and a son by the second. She would be fifty-six or fifty-seven now. I remember her saying that her parents were old and wouldn't understand, that her mother was forty when she had her, and her father over fifty. I thought they were her grandparents when I met them.

She was fifteen or sixteen that winter, and I a year or so older. But I can't help thinking that she's older than her parents now, since they've remained the same age in my head as they were then. Is she too old to understand when her own children giggle and fumble in the dark at the bottom of the stairs? Does she remember, when she hears them whispering, the night we faced each other in a similar darkness, unable to express anything but confusion and self-protective anger, and went our separate ways without so much as a goodbye?

She didn't love me, and I didn't love her, and the light was out at the bottom of the stairs. She came into my arms only to push me away, a woman about to leave her girlhood and a man who was still a boy, both too young to know we were her parents then as we

are her children now, as we stood face to face on the darkened
threshold.

The Eternal Mystery is as mysterious as a dog asleep on the porch with his head resting on his paws. Nothing can disturb him. If you shout, he twitches an ear, maybe rolls over. If you kick him, he sways erect, plods two or three steps to the side, and with a snuffle settles into sleep once more. No reaction—yet we watch him posed like the Sphinx with its head lowered, and stare in fascination as his eyelids flutter, his haunches spasm, and he sprints in place, whimpering one moment and growling the next.

Why does he grumble? Is he dreaming of us? What sounds does he hear inside those ears, winding up from catacombs deep inside his head, where flickering walls echo the words of several singers chanting around a small fire dedicated to the dead? What causes his haunches to spasm and race—a forest of lightning from which there is no escape? And that growl, is he reimagining the daily apprehension that afflicts us all—the implacable shadow that waits at the end of a darkened hall?

THE FINAL EXTINCTION

It was the last one of its kind, of all kinds except their own. They peered at it and stroked it, murmured and nodded.

Now they knew. In the beginning it had not been apparent, in the beginning when the crawlers and flutterers had disappeared. But when the trotters and flyers and slick-sided swoopers through ocean depths had departed, they understood that with each of those passings a part of themselves had vanished, as though each disappearance was the loss of a bodily organ.

Now they knew. They touched the last one of its kind, of all kinds except their own. They no longer poked and prodded it, but with trembling fingers grazed its papery skin, as though tracing a vanished land mass on an ancient map.

Now they knew. As they watched its fluttering gills, they understood that with each extinction they had lost so much of themselves that when this last one sipped its final breath they would become invisible; and then they and their kind would pour through the valleys and mountain passes, howling and moaning for the lost herds.

Moments I Cherish

I cherish those moments between 4 and 5 a.m., when I emerge from sleep to hear the dust chiming around me.

I don't know how long it takes before I realize that the silence woke me, and that the chiming around my bed is the murmuring of the dead.

Have they come for me, that relentless multitude, their robes slipping over the carpet, their hymn so hushed it's almost a hum?

Mostly, those moments occur just before dawn, and I think what has wakened me is the titanic grinding of the earth on its axis as it turns its face and mine toward the light.

But it happens deep in the night as well, and I lie there wide awake, surrounded by the darkness and something else.

Then it's gone—a shiver, a shadow, a departed breath, a premonition that reminds me once again that my bed is a barge, and with neighbors, redwoods, palaces and bees, I'm carried along in a procession streaming toward the light.

THE PHOTO OF PESSOA'S TRUNK

Pessoa's trunk is made of dark wood. It is four feet across and two feet high, and stands open below a bookshelf crowded with books, its inner lid showing the whorls and patterns of the tree it once was. The trunk is filled with manuscripts in manila envelopes —envelopes as anonymous as the book titles on the out-of-focus book shelves above it.

At first, I imagined the old poet was buried beneath the envelopes, his laid-out skeleton like white roots that push bushes and shrubs above the ground—thorny, brittle bushes that hunch and hold fast in a raw winter landscape without snow.

In time, I imagined those roots were really vines that slithered over and under and through the envelopes, squeezing them to powder or damp rot, the words crawling away in all directions in search of mulch or water or wood or anything else that might keep them alive.

Of course, all that was nonsense, tribal fears of wind and darkness. The manuscripts, tucked in their envelopes, are, as befits a trunk, simply the poet's clothes, folded and ready to keep anyone warm, anyone who might need them while walking out alone into the night's anonymous cold.

Reading George Seferis

Last night I read the poems of George Seferis, who has been dead for more than thirty years. In one, he is sitting in a rowboat as it slips past a small island in a bay whose water is like "slain peacocks." He is looking up at the ruins of a fortress where "the sunlight struck diamonds from the walls," searching for a sign, he says, some momento of an ancient king whose black ships had sailed with the Achaian fleet for Troy. He doesn't find the sign or anything else, not even a pottery chip or a rusty helmet flake.

In another poem, he records being at an archaeological dig at dusk on the island of Cyprus when time stopped and a miraculous ascent took place. The workers in the trenches, the swallows like soot skimming just above the fields, clouds in the sky—all were immobile for the moment the young female worker ascended to the heavens like Mary, the Mother of God. Then arms plunged and lifted once again, wings fluttered over stubble, clouds floated by. No one paused to look into the distance, no one turned to whisper to the person next in line, not even the young girl who continued to dig in the waning light, unaware of her miraculous ascension in the poet's mind.

In other poems, written in exile during the war, he broods on the devastation he will find when he returns home, and laments the countrymen he left behind, "their bodies like broken branches."

Seferis' voice was speaking in my ear, a friend who was talking only to me, telling me about incidents that had quickened his breath, excited his sense of life, or made his day a little more meaningful, and that—if he said it right—he thought might do the same for mine.

If he said it right: it was something that simple yet not that simple. It was about the way the words leaned together, clicking against each other like castanets, the consonants at times igniting sparks from one another, the vowels like ball bearings rolling the words inevitably on—and all this created a trembling in the words in the same way a tree standing alone in a field sometimes trembles, the whole tree, all its leaves shaking, although there is no wind, not even a breeze, anywhere in sight. The words were charged with the poet's urgency to speak. No, not an urgency, a necessity that said everything and nothing, that said, in the end, what all poets' words do: "I was here, and each time you read these words, I am here with you."

BACKBONE

for Kirby & Anita Wilkins

My backbone transfixes me. It holds me upright, lodged between my birth and my death. I hang my coat on it when I leave the house and trudge through the wintry streets. And when I return, it is as stiff as the hall clothes-stand where I leave my coat before I stride into the living room.

The old people are gathered in the living room and will not look up. I am surprised that they are there; I am always surprised that they are there. They sit on sofas and easy chairs, jerking threads from their sleeves or performing a fidgety needlework. The heat is enormous and rolls around them—a roomful of spastics who say nothing to each other and where the only sounds are the tapping of the clock and the clicking of the old womens' knitting needles.

As always, the old man with the moustache of white smoke sees me enter. In a moment, he will jump to his feet, shake his fist, shout "Vengeance!" and stand there trembling. As always, silence will wash outward from him and the knitting needles will continue to stutter as if nothing has happened. And as always, I will want to beg the old people's forgiveness, although I won't know why: I will want to kneel before the old man and feel his open hand cover my head like a cap. But also, as always, my back will not bend. *Tomorrow,* I will think, *tomorrow I will try, damn them, really try.* And clenching my teeth, I will turn, buck through the heat, and lurch from the room.

But tonight, before I can move, the old people, led by the old man, rise and approach me, kiss my fingers and lay my hands against their cheeks—a procession of the palsied that passes by without a word, tears flashing in their eyes.

I want to say something, although I don't know what, but they are gone before I can speak.

Alone. The only sounds are the clock tapping and somebody whimpering; and when I realize that I am the person whimpering, I slump to my knees and rock back and forth until my forehead rests on the floor.

Why did I come? Why did the old people leave and I fall to my knees and whimper?

I rise through the heat and sprint toward the door, grabbing my coat from the hall stand.

Outside it is cold and clear. The town seems abandoned. Moonlight slides down the walls of the narrow streets, chalking the domes and roofs, the fishing boats in the harbor, and the hills that surround the town on three sides. Animals snarl beyond the hills, and on a high ridge overlooking the sea, the old people are silhouetted against the sky. Hand in hand, they dance in a line toward the cliff edge, the moonlight sprawling on the black waters below.

In the surrounding houses, children sigh and turn over in sleep.

I shiver: I am transfixed, yet I remain upright. When I return to the house, I hang my coat on the hall clothes-stand and tiptoe into the living room.

"Not Yet"

As children, we hear those words whenever we fidget in our sailor suit or stiff white dress, or when we look up expectantly from the coloring book in papa's car.

It is the answer we get when we creep from bed to ask if Santa Claus has come or if it is New Year's yet, and it is what we are told when we pout on the railroad train that keeps ticking its tongue on the roof of its mouth like sour Aunt Beth, or when we whine in the airplane that has been looking for a place to land ever since taking off.

In classrooms and concert halls, in restaurants and churches, all dragging their bargelike bottoms toward recess or lunch or home-to-bed, "Not yet, not yet," the adults intone again and again, a phrase that is peculiarly theirs and that we realize early on is part of the vocabulary of being grown up.

But when we are grown, we are told the same thing by gunnery sergeants and traffic cops, by sweethearts and boyfriends, husbands and wives.

Everyone, it seems, wants us to practice the patience of monks and nuns, and what we want, what we expect to happen, never seems to occur, until one day we find ourselves telling our children those same words everyone else has said to us.

That's not all. When we are old and look back, we are surprised to find that everything has arrived as it should—wars, weddings, holidays, and years—but somehow they have come and gone without our knowing it, while we've been waiting impatiently for them to happen, as though we had turned away for a moment and missed our bus, and had been left waiting once again, this time for our death. "Still waiting," we think with a smirk, and then we continue as if we had finally won a game or a bet, "I could die today or tomorrow, but I'm not dead now, no—" and through our widening smile two final words slip like drops of honey from our tongue: "not yet."

WHO SAYS WE'RE NOT LUCKY?

An Egyptian airliner plunges into the sea, killing all three hundred aboard. Ten thousand people in various Turkish towns, their apartment buildings toppling in a thunderous quake, are squashed to death as they sleep. Rivers named Mississippi and Yangtze and Danube flood farms and villages, drowning countless animals and humans. In China, an entire city of more than one hundred thousand people collapses into rubble. In Cambodia, three million men, women and children are hacked and shot to death by a political regime, their only memorial acres of white bones littering open fields or poking up from bogs and shallow riverbeds. And in World War II, six of the eleven million people gassed by the Nazis accounted for three out of four of the world's Jews. I, and maybe you, are the fourth, the one who remained alive. Or you're the Turk, the Cambodian, the Chinese. Who says we're not lucky? So far we've been lucky enough to survive.

HEART ATTACK

When I visited my friend in the hospital, he was smiling, his face pale and small against the pillows.

"It was as if God had placed his whole hand on my chest with infinite, loving gentleness," he said. "I've never known such pain."

FOOTNOTES

At a supermarket or a baseball game, in a voting booth knowing that millions of others in similar booths are making the same decisions across the nation, I often think I'm nothing more than a footnote on a yet-to-be-written page. My friends feel the same way.

The momentous battles, championship games, and burning cities are walls of voices, a gibberish of packed-together human sounds that do not so much rise above us as press down on our shoulders and heads.

It's different for generals and presidents. They ride through the glorious gardens of prose, their medal-jingling uniforms and frock coats passing by hedgerows buzzing with the contemplations of insects and shrubs. The dignitaries are on their way to review row after row of troops, each of whom is thinking his own thoughts before he and his fellows march as a regiment into battle on the next page, or into the years between wars where they raise families, contract cancer, and die in solitary rooms. And all the while their gibberish twitters among all the other noises on all the other pages of all the other people come and gone, and only the footnotes remain as a reminder of those who were anonymously here and continued on.

Woodstock, Hiroshima, ransacked Rome. "I was there," is the phrase to describe it. The speaker, whoever he is, licks his lips and stares hollow-eyed beyond our ear.

Superbowl, Thermopylae, Waterloo—most of the time the speaker speaks not so much to authenticate the event as to verify his existence in a specific time and place.

Stalingrad, The Long March, Wounded Knee: the words pile up on the page like bodies left frozen in the snow. One of them, maybe two or three, is identified—Tania Chernova, Liu Chang-fa, Turning Feather—picked from the unmentioned numbers of the living or the dead to stand below the roiling masses as a memorial for the rest.

Auschwitz, Tenochtitlan, Watts in the long hot summer of '65.

Looked at another way, one or two participants volunteer to step from the ranks of anonymity and stand below, as a testimonial that the event described above took place. More important, they stand as proof that unnamed others took part in the event—that you and I were there. And some, through notions of ritual sacrifice, stand apart to bear witness for us all.

And there *is* a sacrifice. For one, the footnote never sees the heavens. The page rises above it, a wall of gibberish, page after page of gibberish like walls of piled bodies blocking out the sky. But the footnote stays, a statue in a deserted city square, while the others, with shrieks and laughter, roam through the streets beyond, searching for the next party or battle or ballgame that, for a moment, will allow them to believe in something other than despair.

Troy, Angkor, Zimbabwe—empty cities for monkeys and slithering vines, whose silence and secrets are punctuated only by the footnote of the archaeologist's shovel digging through time.

The irony in all this is that we long to be footnotes in the end, especially when we find ourselves in a hospital bed or thrown from a car onto a country road. Then we remember the events through which we've steered our lives, events like banners in defeat that swirl downward through the darkness overhead, or spiral like the wings of flaming fighter planes—angelic memories that plummet beyond footnotes, a fiery freefall vanishing into an unwritten night.

THE MOMENT FOR WHICH THERE IS NO NAME

On the sixteenth floor of one of the tall old buildings in the north end of the city, the windows of an apartment look out over the bay. The apartment is empty, the floors and walls bare. There is only a chalked circle on the living room floor. The circle traces the spot where an armchair once stood, an armchair in which an old man regularly sat watching the smokestacks come and go in the harbor in the same way he had watched the swaying forests of masts when he was a boy.

The circle was drawn by the old man's grandson while the child's parents were supervising the movers.

Tomorrow the new tenants will arrive, and before they move in, they will clean the apartment. In the course of their cleaning, they will erase the chalk.

That is the moment for which there is no name.

ELEGY FOR THINGS TO COME

1.

There must be many staircases under the earth: moss-soft, fibrous, narrow and steep—a mulch of brown leaves packed together.

The dead climb back and forth on these stairs. It's an arduous journey, but they don't mind. When they're called, they come.

Alone in single rooms when alive, ignored by the noisy crowd, many of them have achieved a stature they could never have imagined.

We think of them milling around in buried cities, drinking the blood of the living when we sleep, or taunting us with pranks that ruffle our afternoons. But they watch over us, guiding us around corners, listening to our sorrows and fears in the night, and ushering us into each new day.

This is another of my grandfather's tales about a town on the other side of the world, where buildings were pounded to rubble in an almost forgotten war, and no one was left to tell the secrets of the dead to the living so the dead would remain alive.

2.

I had a friend who grew up in an English mansion. There were paintings in all the halls: landscapes, battles, the hunt, but mostly long-faced ancestors with imperious expressions, wearing waistcoats, doublets, and shimmering gowns. They were standing inside the walls, my friend said, and he imagined them climbing down from their places every night and trudging through hidden passageways to moldering, candlelit kitchens, where they ate and drank and gossiped about the living they'd seen come and go all day. My friend would never venture downstairs after the lights were out. He knew the frames were empty, he said, as if they were windows admitting an endless white light that lay everywhere beyond the house.

3.

Death is a place far to the north, where the telephone lines carrying our questions and whisperings are buried in the drifting snow.

The wires neither spark nor twitch.

No puddles seethe from their heat.

They just disappear into the snow like so much fishing line that someone left an hour or a year or a century ago, and that deep below passing fish may nibble on before they flutter into the enclosing dark.

4.

All we can hope for in the end is to be a face with an unchanging expression on a painting smoldering in soot-smeared rubble, or to resemble a figure among painted flowers on a water jug who a young girl, just before she turns toward home, traces for a moment with her fingertips.

ANOTHER BITE FROM THE COSMIC APPLE

Ptolemy, Copernicus, Galileo, Kepler, Newton...Newton? Newton-Schmoonton. Let me tell you how the universe really works.

The universe is an apple. The outer hemispheres are open to bombardments of X-rays and light rays and gamma rays from beyond the finite; gelatinous nebulae like giant amoebas; crusty, twittering microbes that spin from the darkness to gouge the surface or brush past it, leaving bruises or brown spots—all those events and manifestations we'll never experience, which assail the outside of the apple as it sits in the fruit bowl in God's kitchen. So why worry? Who cares? Forget about it.

Under the skin is the universe we know: dense white matter like compressed champagne that makes up most of inner space. But this matter is such an intense white we see it as black shot through with golden droplets of cider, a sort of biological compensation to protect us from what Professor Lucien Russell called "interstellar snow blindness."

We live in the elongated caverns in the center of this apple, like Eskimos in ice caves, wearing our skins like clumsy, padded outer garments.

It's not that we're cold. We're oppressed by all the pressure hemming us in on all sides, as if we lived in an igloo in the center of an iceberg.

You hear what I'm saying? The density of the atmosphere is unbearable at times—all that whiteness we experience as blackness hovering around us, and the droplets of cider glittering like solidified points of light at the tips of stalactites hanging out of reach so high above.

And what are we doing here, anyway? That's the question,

Magister Ptolemy. Are we just hanging around, Canon Copernicus, waiting for someone to pick up the apple from the fruit bowl, chomp into it and chew us to nothingness, unaware not only that we're here but that, Signor Galileo, we are at the core of the eternal mystery, dancing and shouting with glee, despite our imprisonment, Herr Kepler, dancing and singing even in our sorrows and frustrations, Sir Isaac, the vibrations from these caverns resonating throughout the entire apple?

BLINKING

You've got to love life so much that you don't want to miss a moment of it, and pay such close attention to whatever you're doing that each time you blink you can hear your eyelashes applauding what you've just seen.

In each eye there are more than eighty eyelashes, forty above and forty below, like forty pairs of arms working, eighty pairs in both eyes, a whole audience clapping so loud you can hardly bear to listen.

One hundred sixty hands batter each other every time you blink. "Bravo!" they call, "Encore! Encore!"

Paralyzed in a hospital bed, or watching the cold rain from under a bridge—remember this.

THE FIELD

I loved to lie in the grass when I was a boy. I'd lie on my back, looking up through the tree branches as the sky flew away in its blue and white robes.

But mostly I'd lie on my stomach, peering through the forests of grass. Soon the ants would arrive, or a beetle on his way to somewhere else.

The longer I lay still, the more birds and animals would appear and the more I would feel less like myself and more like the field, an expanse where bees and robins settled for a moment before flying on.

Now I sense rustlings and quiverings everywhere around me, as if tribes from the same valley were getting ready for a journey. The tree branches resemble a spider web in which I am caught, or the sky is, and when I turn over, the ants are already there, and behind them the beetles picking their way over stones.

There are moments I can hear the weeds unfurling their wings and the grass sliding upward, nudging aside acorns and leaves.

At such times I think this is all I can hope for. Not that the plants or animals have come to greet me, but that they don't even know I am there.

AT PEACE

Some nights the universe is a black stone millions of miles tall and eons wide, and balancing on its surface somewhere, a luminous drop of water is poised like a bird's egg on top of a black monument. But there are other nights when the black monolith's internal structure relaxes, and the drop of water sinks like a glowing pearl through its depths, illuminating veins and root ends, tiny skulls with empty eye sockets, fossils of ferns and fish fins, and I am at peace.

WORDS BEFORE SLEEP

Tonight I have acknowledged once and for all that my bones are nothing more than a roller coaster in a seedy amusement park, and whoever/whatever I am huddles inside its shadow.

The scaffolding creaks around me in the dark, yet even as I watch old newspapers and empty candy wrappers skip by like children on Halloween, I'm stirred by a sense of freedom I've never felt before.

To be imprisoned in the self is to identify all that is not me by all that is, much as a carpenter takes comfort as well as pleasure in seeing the structures he's built, although he doesn't own them.

Dark wind, you are as much my breath as the universe's. Let us hum a duet to celebrate the passing year.

INCIDENT FROM THE DAY OF THE DEAD

Miguel told me he had been home alone for two hours, studying. It was in Guanajuato when he was twelve years old, on the Day of the Dead, and his mother and sisters had gone to tidy his father's and grandparents' graves.

He didn't remember why he looked from his book on the dining room table to the sideboard in the corner, where his baby sister had surrounded the makeshift altar with the candies his grandmother liked so much and the small dark cigars his father and grandfather were so fond of. It was probably a sound of some sort, he said, a chair creaking maybe. But when he looked, there was his father, turned the other way, holding a cigar under his nose, sideways, like a flute, sniffing the length of it as he did when he was alive.

The old man was so intent on the cigar, his face serious, that he didn't notice Miguel at first. He was sitting on a dining room chair, in the black suit he had been buried in, leaning toward the altar as if he had just picked up the cigar. Then he tensed and a moment later turned toward Miguel, and they sat that way, looking at each other across the table in the late afternoon light. And that's how Miguel knew, he said, that only a table separates the living from the dead.

"What did you do then?" I asked.

Miguel shook his head.

We had been talking for hours about one thing and another, sipping beer at my kitchen table, while the household slept and the night wind buffeted the tiny house on the northern California coast. Our talk had wandered onto the brushes we had had with the dead, and he had told this story about his father, and now it was clear he had said all he intended to say.

"That's it?" I asked. "Nothing more?"

"No. Nothing."

We sat in silence for several moments. *Just as he and his father had*, I thought, and I said aloud to continue the conversation, "How long did you sit that way?"

He shrugged. "My mother and sisters returned soon after."

"And he was gone then?"

He clenched his jaw and looked past me toward the window.

I knew that if I continued my questioning I would be invading a reserve in him that I had learned to respect, and I must admit that I was too timid or unwilling to hurl myself at the barricade of facial expressions he had thrown up between us, and there the matter ended, although I felt that I had somehow failed, failed in the same way Miguel and his father had failed with each other.

At the same time, I felt that the incident wasn't finished. Miguel had told me the story, and somehow the story and the telling and what had just occurred at my kitchen table were now joined in a single event. It made no difference if Miguel and I never spoke of the incident again, or if my insistence had destroyed our friendship, which, I'm relieved to say, it did not.

It was as though the story told me in a California kitchen by a middle-aged man about an incident from his childhood in Mexico now included me, was somehow mine as much as it was his, and continued from that point, having less and less to do with our friendship, or even us. His reticence and my timidity, both our failures, and his failure with his father and his father's failure with him, were what the story was about.

And now, dear reader, just as I became part of the story Miguel told me, so you have become part of the story, too. It is as if we sit across from each other at a kitchen table, although I am no longer here and possibly wrote these words years ago. I may no longer even be alive. You, however, read these words as if I am sitting here with you, and that has allowed me to include you in the tale, a tale whose telling beyond this point I am either unwilling or unable to provide.

THE LIBRARY

When I die I will be a book on a shelf in the library, and this notion doesn't bother me. I look forward to leaning against Melville and Montaigne, and I can't wait to stand in the ranks shoulder to shoulder with Rabelais, Sterne, and Twain laughing with them and pausing now and again to listen entranced to sonorous Willie S.

Think of it: Cervantes and his knight proclaim the difficulties of chivalry a dozen rows above me, while next to them Chekhov sighs among his landowners and peasants and shakes his head. Just below them, Dostoyevsky rants about salvation and guilt, while on the shelf over mine Li Po, intoning words of reverence, raises a wine cup to the moon, and, dozens of rows farther down, Whitman, enraptured by it all, bellows his exaltation.

What more can one wish for than to be buried in such a mausoleum, where my friends and I will live forever, better prepared for eternity than a pharaoh in his tomb, since the words in books will provide us with all the earthly goods we'll need to live a luxurious afterlife.

Meanwhile, here, now, the words in books plant trees, launch rivers through forests and plains, and build cities crowded with skyscrapers and tenements. But what if the world, I often wonder, is only a ball of light we populate with phantoms of the mind and flickering longings of the heart? Then this edifice of books I choose to be my crypt exists only in my head and will not outlast the moment of my death. Not even a vacant lot, littered with fluttering pages and toppled walls, will remain.

That possibility doesn't disturb me: I've assumed from the start that the library continually disappears, as if, like an enchanted castle, it is under a spell from which it can be resurrected only when a boy or girl, man or woman, finds and steps inside its hidden entrance—that secret door which is always close at hand, yet, until we recognize it, we think is nothing more than the cover of a book.

Morton Marcus was born in New York City in 1936 and has lived in California since 1961. He is the author of seven books of poetry and one novel, including *The Santa Cruz Mountain Poems, Pages From a Scrapbook of Immigrants*, and *When People Could Fly*. He has published over four-hundred poems in such literary journals as *The Denver Quarterly, Ploughshares, TriQuarterly*, and *The Prose Poem: An International Journal*, and his work has been selected to appear in more than seventy-six anthologies in the United States, Europe, and Australia. Later in 2002 Creative Arts Book Company will publish his *Shouting Down the Silence*, a new book of verse poems, and in 2003 the same publisher will bring out *Bear Prints*, Marcus's collected verse poems. Marcus has read his poems and taught writing workshops in colleges across the country, and he is co-host of a poetry radio show. A long interview with him on the prose poem appeared on the March/April 2001 issue of *The Bloomsbury Review*. A film historian and critic as well as poet, Marcus lives in Santa Cruz.

THE MARIE ALEXANDER POETRY SERIES

Editor: Robert Alexander

Volume 5
Moments Without Names:
New & Selected Prose Poems
Morton Marcus

Volume 4
Whatever Shines
Kathleen McGookey

Volume 3
Northern Latitudes
Lawrence Millman

Volume 2
Your Sun, Manny
Marie Harris

Volume 1
Traffic
Jack Anderson

—Forthcoming—
The Blue Dress
Alison Townsend
Spring 2003